Bedroom Ideas

Bedroom Ideas

by the Editors of
Hudson Home Guides

BANTAM/HUDSON IDEA BOOKS

New York, New York • Los Altos, California

BEDROOM IDEAS

A Bantam Book/published in association
with Hudson Home Publications.
First printing December 1976
Second printing August 1977

Executive Editor, Robert J. Dunn; Book Editor, Sandra L.
Beggs; Project Editor, Joseph F. Schram; Associate Editors,
Robert Agee, Oriana Mead; Art Director, Carolyn M. Thompson;
Cover Design & Illustrations, Kenneth Vendley; Book Design,
Annette T. Yatovitz; Graphics, Dean Holmer.

Cover Photo, Idaka; Designers: Brenda Bruce and Arlene Semel.

ISBN 0-553-01044-1

Published simultaneously in the United States and Canada

Bantam Books are published by Bantam Books, Inc. Its trade-
mark, consisting of the words "Bantam Books" and the por-
trayal of a bantam, is registered in the United States Patent
Office and in other countries. Marca Registrada. Bantam
Books, Inc., 666 Fifth Avenue, New York, New York 10019.

Printed in the United States of America.
Library of Congress catalog card number 76-41027.

Contents

1 Planning

Planning a bedroom can be a most pleasant adventure, one that releases one's innermost desires for securing a private haven of quiet relaxation, an inner sanctum to be enjoyed upon demand. Or, if the room is to be used by guests or other members of the family, it can be a splendid offering of comfort in surroundings conducive to slumber, quiet reading or just plain relaxing!

Your first step in bedroom planning, as in all other home planning, should involve the determination of what you really want, who will use the room, how big it can be, what style you wish to follow, what furniture will be needed, the best utilization of space and room layout, etc. Asking yourself penetrating questions at the outset will insure that you've included all the necessities and extras you desire.

Keep in mind that this important space is just as important for day in, day out living as any other in the home and should be treated as such. As much as one third of your life is spent in the bedroom, which is probably more than you spend in any other room in your home. It's here where you can get away from the chores and troubles of the day and find peaceful comfort. It's here where you can rekindle your spirit, renew your energies and be totally you. Yet, here is also a setting that will be viewed often by others as they pass by. With the door open and everything in its place, the bedroom can be a unique expression of your style of living, your zest for life, the personal you. Bedroom planning should be a personal extension of the basics offered in this book.

Photographer: Kent Oppenheimer

Planning Basics

Unfortunately for many, bedroom planning is something that someone else has done for them, and in many cases the results are highly unsatisfactory and undesirable. The space is too small, the room has windows in the worst imaginable places, doors open the wrong way, there's only one possible placement for the bed and no chance of using the next larger size bed, closet space isn't sufficient and the total setting is as restful as rush hour on the freeway. For those who have the opportunity to do their own bedroom planning, either through remodeling or new construction, the opportunities are great and the possibilities of success even greater — greater, that is, if sound planning basics are understood and followed.

To begin with, it's been determined that a master or primary bedroom for two persons should have at least one uninterrupted wall space of at least 10 feet, and at least one window with sill height not more than 48 inches above the floor and providing not less than 5 square feet of opening with no dimension less than 22 inches. Entry doors should be a minimum 32 inches wide and closet doors in two-person bedrooms should be no less than 5 feet wide and 80 inches high. Inswinging entry doors in the bedroom are best placed 2 feet from a corner rather than in the middle of a wall, permitting placement of furniture in the 2-foot space. Ceilings generally are 8 feet high, but a minimum acceptable height is 7 feet 6 inches in areas such as attics. Secondary bedrooms require a minimum "least wall dimension" of 8 feet, but more space is desirable for greater flexibility of furniture arrangement.

Being the largest element of the bedroom, the bed itself should receive primary consideration, both in its selection and placement. Antique and older beds sometimes are larger than newer ones manufactured to accommodate the following mattress sizes:

- King Size   75x80"
- Queen Size   60x80"
- Longster Full   54x80"
- Longster Twin   39x80"
- Full   54x75"
- Twin   39x75"
- Crib   27x48"

If you are planning to use a water bed instead of the conventional box springs and mattress, keep in mind that the standard size unit will weigh in the neighborhood of a ton when filled and perhaps will require additional floor framing support.

Regardless of bed style, there are three desirable minimum space dimensions that should be maintained in bed placement:

- It should be 40 inches from the foot to any wall, furniture face or closet front.
- It should be 28 inches away from a sidewall

on which no furniture is located, or 40 inches from a sidewall on which furniture or a closet is located.

- It should be 28 inches apart from another bed in instances where twin beds are used in the room parallel to each other.

These clearances will afford necessary space for cleaning the floor, making the bed, opening doors and drawers, dressing and gaining access to windows and closets.

Other furniture used in the bedroom is manufactured in a range of sizes without a fixed standard for given units. However, there are some "averages" which may prove helpful in gaining a feel for space requirements. These include:

- Night stands are from 14 to 26 inches across the face and 15 to 20 inches in depth.
- Dressers and chests are 25 to 72 inches wide and 18 to 22 inches front-to-back.
- Overstuffed armchairs are 24 to 34 inches wide

the desired color — this is why you see walnut, birch or mahogany in a variety of wood tones. A glaze or shellac seals the color permanently. Several coats of lacquer are applied and sanded, then hand-rubbed to the proper gloss, be it bright or soft. The most popular finish today is the close-to-the-wood finish, a dull-rubbed treatment giving the utmost importance to the wood's natural grain. Other finishes include waxing, liming (pigment rubbed into heavily grained wood, such as oak, to emphasize pattern), and antiquing. The latter "ages" the wood's appearance by affecting small darkened areas, or by a process called "highlighting" which imitates wear at prominent rounded sections.

Inlay, parquetry, and marquetry are all ancient art forms, using rare woods and figures to achieve unusual decorative effects. Inlay is generally a trim, with a wood such as ebony set into a groove to provide an exotic note. Parquetry is the arrangement of wood pieces in geometric form, such as squares or herringbone strips. Grains or wood tones are alternated to afford contrast. Marquetry is the "illustrative" use of woods in larger pieces, and may utilize the matching process of veneering with similar figures side by side or "mirroring" two sucessive wood slices, a process called book matching. Marquetry is seen in bedroom cabinet doors, table tops and other large surfaces where importance can be given to imposing wood figures.

Wallcoverings, floors and carpets, window treatments, furniture selection, lighting and electronics, fabric choices, ceilings, doors, storage — they're all basic considerations in planning a bedroom that will withstand the test of time.

Sketches: Kenneth Vendley

and about 22 inches deep; straight chairs are 15 to 22 inches wide and equally deep.

Desks, occasional tables, ottomans, chaise lounges and other furniture are common components of most bedrooms where space permits.

In buying furniture for the bedroom it is helpful to understand that most solid wood furniture pieces are Early American, traditionally made from boards of maple, cherry or birch. However, the overwhelming majority of fine furniture is made from veneered hardwood plywood for resistance to warping or buckling, and to afford the use of the most beautifully figured hardwoods where they are visible and may be admired. Veneering is a venerable art, used throughout the centuries by such masters as Chippendale. A single hardwood, veneered on surfaces and solid in legs, is called "genuine walnut" or other wood, as appropriate.

Today's modern finishes for bedroom furniture begin with bleaching or staining the wood to create

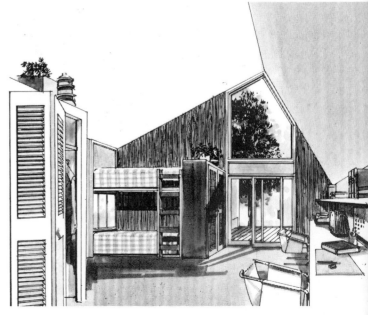

Planning Basics

In planning your bedroom design, the first most obvious question is what sort of function you want it to serve. Perhaps you have an extra room in the house (even an unused attic) you'd like to use as bedroom/guest room/den. Maybe you'd like to expand your master bedroom to create the ultimate suite including bath, sitting area, and garden deck. If you don't want to change the bedroom structurally, a simple furniture rearrangement and new color scheme could help perk up an average size room. Whatever type of room you want, be sure to evaluate its existing qualities carefully to take full advantage of its potential.

Color should always be a basic consideration in bedroom planning and design — and basic red, white and blue schemes are perennially stimulating. The townhouse den/guest room below, by interior designer Peg Walker, brings beach house flair and seaside hardiness to the city home. Colors from the carpet are carried to the vinyl-coated, fiberglass Peruvian Stripe window shades which are hung reverse-roll within the reveals of handsome 19th century windows. The looped hemshapes of the

shades were cut to accommodate white rod-shade-pulls that accentuate the architectural flavor. Extra shade cloth faces the air conditioner to play down its distracting brownness without interfering with its operation.

Small space needn't be a drawback in bedroom planning, as is proved in the room shown below. Designer Carleton Varney has turned a long narrow area with minimal light into a room that's sunny, bright and spacious in appearance. Virtually every surface is sunlit yellow — the walls, the carpeting and the fabric background. The repetition of one tone blurs the distinctions between walls and floor and thus gives a more open feeling. Purest white touches moldings, quilt and shutters to heighten the sparkle of light. Furniture of white wicker and a Chinese garden seat lack any heaviness and relate to the out-of-doors. Two well-planned closets make a niche for the bed and hold all of the clothing, eliminating the need for additional furniture which would cramp room space. By keeping the floor uncluttered, space has been used for a seating area. With an eye toward budget, old furniture was cov-

ered in a coordinating fabric, while a fresh coat of paint for old porch furniture saved the wicker. Wicker tables and flower baskets complement the setting, and the quilt, a family inheritance, finishes the room. The artificial illumination is derived from a ceiling fixture and a pair of wall-mounted lamps which swing easily to accommodate reading in bed. The headboard is an integral part of the bed itself.

A master bedroom should be the epitome of convenience and comfort. This is the one room with responsibilities only to its occupants, which means that here's the opportunity to surround yourself with colors, patterns, and furnishings that truly delight you. You can go romantic, exotic or however you wish, without worrying about the needs or preferences of other members of the family or guests.

Creating a fresh mood is the easiest of all especially if space is no limitation, as in the situation below. Designed by Mary O'Connor of Barrows Studio of Interior Design, Phoenix, Arizona, the two-level setting includes distinctive areas for luxurious relaxation, sleeping and bathing-dressing. This private retreat tastefully combines the key elements of a successful master bedroom: natural but controlled lighting via shuttered windows and doors; artificial illumination produced by wall-mounted, suspended and table fixtures; comfortable furniture for any time of the day or night; plants that add a touch of refreshing green; floor covering that is soft to the touch; and accessories that blend with and complement every other element.

A child's bedroom should always be more than just that! The awake hours spent here often will equal sleeping time, especially in climates where weather sometimes keeps youngsters indoors. Planning a child's room can be as much fun as occupying the finished room. Memories of childhood quickly surface as you conserve as much floor space as possible for games, or even build them right into the scene as shown below in this child's bedroom designed by Margot Condon which incorporates a bright checkerboard floor for two young brothers. Keep in mind that children have very special interests. Let them help in planning the decor for their own room and you'll find it becomes a special personal retreat to them.

Photographer: Max Eckert

Photographer: Dick Sharpe

Space Planning

The bedroom, like any other room in a home, should make the most of the alloted space. What is done design-wise between four walls is the challenge extended to the home owner with the assistance of builder, architect and designer. A small, well-planned room often can better accommodate more furniture than a larger room with poorly planned furniture arrangement, window locations and door openings. Doors are best located in corners of the room, with windows in opposite corners not more than 4 feet above the floor and with no dimension less than 22 inches. Closets should likewise command a corner location when possible, with floor-to-ceiling access to a depth of 24 inches for maximum storage potential. Determination of the desired bed-mattress is the first step in calculating the amount of space available for bedroom "planning". These units require space as follows: Crib 27x48", Twin 39x75", Full 54x75", Queen 60x80", King 75x80". Headboards, of course, add length.

With these standard mattress sizes, it can be determined which are possible and which is best for the basic utilization of available space. Keep in mind that full-bed clearances should provide 28 inches of space from bed to side wall, 40 inches from foot of bed to wall, closet or furniture, and 40 inches of space from opposite bedside to wall, closet or face of furniture. In twin bed arrangements, the 40-inch foot and one side measurements again are preferred, with 28 inches between beds and a minimum of 4 inches from a plain bed wall.

Bed location
Below: Head-to-head placement of twin beds on a single built-in wood platform saves valuable floor space in this bedroom shared by two young brothers. Equal-sized, floor-to-ceiling fixed glass panels flank the sliding glass door unit which opens onto a small redwood deck. The compartmentalized storage unit attached to the redwood paneled wall affords ample space for books, trophies and the like, plus slide-out storage boxes for other items. The combination redwood telephone stand/bed divider is fully accessible from either side.

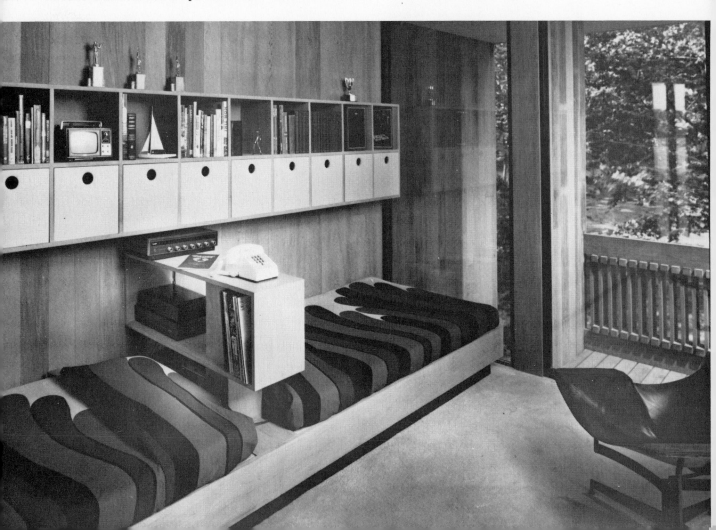

Right: This homeowner's desire to use a small bedroom as a sewing center resulted in creation of a sleeping alcove in what was formerly a wardrobe closet with sliding doors. The original door frame was maintained and a platform constructed with matching floor molding. Closet rods were installed in the alcove framework (as well as in the window opening) for curtains in a companion fabric to the vinyl acrylic wallcovering which affords a timely and timeless floral design throughout the room.

Below: Corner placement of the bed in this master bedroom maximizes usable floor space and provides an uninterrupted view of the ocean via the nearly floor-to-ceiling porthole-style fixed window. The bed is suspended from heavy ceiling beams as part of the waterfront decor. Next to the bed is a sliding panel display of coastline maps that slides across the window for full privacy. The wood deck ceiling and plywood paneled walls keep maintenance to a minimum. Lounger in the foreground is wicker with a fur throw piece and colorful pillows.

Space Planning

Bed 'n' Bath

Along with planning the bedroom area itself, consider locating a bathroom within near proximity. The bedroom and bathroom go nearly hand in hand, and the closer they are the more convenient it will make your daily routine. A part of each other yet totally private, the restful bed n' bath below utilizes a platform approach for both units. Designer David Poisal of Simmons Company has set the bed on a recessed lighted platform to create the effect of floating on light and air. The bathtub, fashioned in mosaic tile, has a step-up platform carpeted like the balance of the room. It may be entered from either side where integral safety rails help assure accident-free movement. The bath itself can be closed off with nearly sheer white curtains suspended from a ceiling track. Another ceiling track permits the placement of flood light fixtures anywhere along the track. The common wall for this bedroom/bath combination is patterned in gray and salmon on white to complement the gray and white tiles used for the side and countertop of the vanity and tub. Mauve silk pillows add comfort and serve as a headboard.

Room for Reading

The solitary enjoyment of a good book takes on further pleasure when the reading is done in the privacy of one's bedroom before a warm fire. Here the master suite includes the elegance of provincial furnishings and the warmth of both fireplace and surrounding paneling, built-in bookcases and paneled doors. The fabric-covered doors add further softness to the warm-toned cabinets and softness of floor covering, while the bookcase interior in maroon creates a pleasing contrast and is repeated in the lap robe. Use of space is well conceived, with the double doors opening into the unused space at bedside making for easy flow throughout the room. The vivid blue and white bed quilt is complemented by the cushioning of the fireside chairs, while the reddish color of the bookcase interior is reflected in the trim of the ladder-back lounge chairs and ottoman. Accessories on the mantel add a further dash of maroon, blue and white. Lighting fixtures throughout the room are dimmer-controlled to permit dialing the desired amount of illumination. Designer: Mary Gold.

Layout Lounge

An enclosed porch off the master bedroom of this San Francisco home was made an integral part of the room itself by surplanting the original interior wall with a handsome archway. The framework is surfaced with painted latticework to enhance the garden-style setting high above the city with a re-circulating waterfall adding to the tranquil atmosphere. The lounge placement affords the user a magnificent view of the city by the Golden Gate, yet does not block the same view from the master bed on the other side of the arches. Resilient flooring in a brick pattern blends well with bedroom carpeting. Designer: George Livermore, AIBD.

Correspondence Center

The privacy and quiet of a bedroom make it an excellent location for a correspondence center where one can devote full attention to the fine art of communicating. This man's retreat combines the delicate, graceful lines of a wrought iron headboard with the massiveness of a large metal sculpture and the clean lines of a plastic laminate desk top. Furniture throughout the room ranges across several style periods including contemporary, creating a pleasant sitting/sleeping situation. The cubical bed-side stand includes clear plastic tubes for current magazines waiting to be read. Designer: Dwight Goldblatt, Riverside, California.

Photographer: Karl Riek (above)

Photographer: Harold Davis (below)

Boudoir Breakfast

Even small bedrooms can include that "something extra" such as a window-corner breakfast area. Strategic placement of two nightstands at the foot of the bed creates an automatic show and store space in an often ignored spot. The natural lighting is softened with sheer curtains and the entire area can be closed off from view with the striped floor-to-ceiling curtains. Walls of this room are painted in a dark gloss color to accentuate the attractive corner eating arrangement. Flooring in durable vinyl features a geometric pattern in light and dark tones to further expand the room visually. The rice white furniture displays well against the dark walls.

Restful Workshop

Truly a "get-away-from-it-all" place, this attic hideaway lets the lady of the house work and relax in total quiet and privacy. Plexiglas framing supports a day bed framed by the roof shape and highlighted by a decorative wallcovering following the structural lines. The dormer area has been utilized for a shaped butcher block counter surface that extends into the sewing machine platform. The same countertop material is used for the pedestal table. Adjustable lighting fixtures solve the often-difficult problem of correct illumination for the visibility needed in such hobbies as sewing, stitchery, and fashion design.

A Working Headboard

The working headboard continues to draw the interest and attention of furniture designers who believe it should do more than simply prop up a few pillows. This clean-line unit has both lift-up and swing-down face panels that turn beauty into function — as a pillow support for reading and as shelving for morning coffee. Aside from full-width, concealed storage compartments, the unit also provides a handy top shelf. Architect: Chester Widom.

Compact Laundry Convenience

A bedroom closet sometimes can be put to further use as a compact laundry. The automatic washer shown here at the lower level is but 21 inches wide and deep, and only 36 inches high. It's on casters and can be moved out from the closet for easier loading and unloading. The automatic dryer shown at eye-level measures 21 inches wide, 18¾ inches deep and 28½ inches high. It's specifically designed for inside exhaustion. It can also be wall mounted.

Cozy Corner

In keeping with the trend towards a more spacious bedroom suite, it's only natural that a fireplace be considered to round off the sense of coziness that can make the bedroom such a comforting place. The elegant bedroom shown at right illustrates what a nice addition a fireplace can be. Located on a corner wall, you can almost imagine yourself nestled beside it. Designers: Brenda Bruce and Arlene Semel, Chicago, Illinois.

Photographer: Glen Allison (above)

Photographer: Idaka (right

2 Definable Designs

This montage of sparkling bedrooms is representative of the wide variety of designs available to the homeowner who lets his imagination soar. Reading from top left, clockwise are:

The Garden Bedroom extends sleeping and sitting areas to the out-of-doors, making the lush greenery a basic part of the decorative scheme. Here designer Carole Eichen for Grant Corp. Developers used plastic panels and redwood framing to create a deck greenhouse.

The Tight Space Bedroom makes the best of a limited area wherever it may be. Designer Charles Foltz used this corner niche to provide a guest bed in a tropical setting, enhanced by bamboo wallcovering and distinctive fabric patterns.

The Attic Retreat by designers Sharon Meadows and Kay Brewer features a curved theme introduced to soften strong architectural lines. The 79-inch diameter bed is covered with a furry throw and piled with pillows.

The Guest Bedroom with its twin four-posters, combines the elegance of wood paneling with frilly white fabrics used for the bed covers. Designer: Price McNutt, ASID.

The Convertible Bedroom makes use of major space for more than a single purpose. Here designer Elizabeth Hodgkin, ASID, has placed an elegant four-poster canopy bed in a corner where it can be used for additional seating.

Photographer: Max Eckert (bottom)

Photographer: Max Eckert

The Master Suite

"A home within-a-home" might well be the proper definition of a master bedroom suite. It should be a place where the occupants can free themselves of all other activities in the house to enjoy the comforts, privacy and serenity that should be theirs alone. The master suite is a distinct area of the home with responsibilities only to the occupants — an area free from the usual decorating dogmas. You can surround yourself with colors, patterns, furnishings and conveniences that truly delight you. Increased accent is being placed on daytime living within the suite. Luxurious bathing facilities frequently include a sunken tub or garden bath equipped with a whirlpool, sauna or even nearby deck hot tub. Grooming centers include well-lighted and movable mirrors, shampoo lavatories and other dressing table luxuries. Space is provided for daytime lounging or relaxing in a comfortble chair with a good book. There's a small table for serene morning coffee and, perhaps, a fireplace for watching while sipping a nightcap. Controlled lighting, television, stereo, radio, telephone, treasured objets d' art — they can all be a part of the master suite and yours alone to enjoy.

Transformation of existing space into a new setting is often the means of obtaining a master suite. Here designer Robert Hutchinson removed all existing walls and the ceiling of a San Francisco Victorian flat and rebuilt the ceiling to a soaring 22-foot height, supported by Douglas fir beams. A fireplace was added and heavily-stained Douglas fir was used for the bed frame, windows, doors and wall trim, the height of each concluding at the same point to unify the room without up-and-down breaks. The furnishings include an early 18th century walnut desk, a late 17th century William and Mary oak table, a 17th century Italian chest of drawers, a tufted-leather Turkish chair from the Teddy Roosevelt era and animal horns dating to the mid-19th century.

Master Suite

Many existing homes contain "hidden" or unused space that can be put to use for a variety of "bonus room" purposes. In this Southern California home, architect designer Ralph Sias went to the attic to plan and construct a new master suite for the owners. Located largely above an attached two-car garage, the space was totally unused at the start and then transformed into a delightful, all-wood haven complete with bedroom, bath, separate lavatory, sewing center, built-in bar, television stereo entertainment wall, and home office. Sias executed his own plans and designs, including constructing the built-ins as a "complete labor of love".

Below: The center area of the new suite is 7'8" at its highest point, sloping to 5' at the walls. Existing ceiling rafters were used to support runners to which Sias nailed clear 1x4" cedar boards. Special framing was used to create a skylight-like appearance for built-in overhead lighting. The treatment was carried over to lighting above the triangular-shaped lavatory which has an all-teak countertop finished with six coats of urethane. Opposite the lavatory is a 6x8' sewing center with built-in sewing machine, workspace and storage. On the opposite side of the sewing unit is a built-in bar complete with small refrigerator and sink.

Left: The bedroom section of the master suite is 12' wide and 26' long and includes a natural-lighting skylight. The 1x4" clear cedar boards are used in three directions in this room, including a herringbone treatment in the niche built for the headboard. The nightstands are built into the wall, with space between for a king-size bed. A chair at the bedroom desk and the bed are the only two pieces of freestanding furniture in the entire suite. Flooring is a high-low shag carpeting, except in the bathroom near the water closet and in the 3x5' shower which can be dammed to use as a Roman tub. These bath surfaces are ceramic tile.

Below: Directly opposite the master bed is this cedar entertainment storage wall, equipped with television and stereo controls. The television is set upon a pull-out Lazy Susan which makes it possible to view the unit from anywhere in the room. The stereo has two speakers each in bedroom, sewing center and bathroom. The built-in storage cabinets again have a teak countertop surface, the right-angle of which is a desk with additional drawer storage. Architect Sias used foil-backed batt insulation for ceiling, walls and floor. All decorative pulls and knobs are wood, in keeping with the walls, ceilings and cabinetry.

Photographer: Richard Fish

Master Suite

Eighteenth century furnishings abound in this English Country bedroom designed by Ella-Mae Manwarring, ASID. The sophisticated citron yellow chinoiserie pattern selected for the walls provides a historical setting for a mahogany bed with turned posts, an antique cherrywood Italian setee, a crewel English wing chair, and an 18th century Chippendale desk chair. Accessories atop the chest include an antique Bible stand and a Danish scale with apples to complement the Italian apple painting in oils above. Solid panel shutters are used for the recessed window treatment. A William of Orange chandelier is appropriate to the setting and augments the table lamp illumination. Flooring is dark oak partially covered with a Belgian needlepoint area carpet.

Photographer: Kent Oppenheimer

The rich beauty of natural pine helped to transform a plain room with open roof framing into this airy beach-side master suite. Large wood beams were fabricated with the knotty material to add more emphasis to the ceiling and highlight the master bed and sliding glass door areas. The non-bearing beams are put to use for book storage. Designed by Campbell-La Rocca for Arthur Shermans, the room has a second built-in bed used as a daytime couch. Both beds have built-in night-stands which provide additional storage space. The master bed's headboard features a dark-toned wood carving, contrasted by light-toned roll-down wood blinds at the bedside window overlooking the ocean. The suite includes a wood-burning fireplace.

Photographer: Elyse Lewin

Master Suite

Left: A small bedroom in this home was expanded from the dark beam toward the garden to provide a master suite with a porch-like seating area. Interior designer Ron Collier selected an antique brass bed and added a canopy made of new brass drapery hardware. The washable sheeting material used for cover and bed curtains is banded with brown and beige material. The Victorian sofa and wing chair are of the English Country period.

Opposite: Dramatic geometric angles defined by wood beams and vertical application of narrow-width tongue-and-groove paneling create a delightful framework for this master suite. A distinctive painted iron headboard adds its own decorative touch to the classical lines of antique furniture used throughout the room. Adjoining the marble-topped chest of drawers is a floral print upholstered chaise lounge that adds a spark of color.

Below: Large, custom-made etegeres flanking the bed in this master suite offer instant control of telephone answering equipment, television and stereo units, and room illumination. The headboard is antiqued carved wood affixed to the wall beneath swing-out reading lamps. Plantation shutters are used for light and privacy control. Just inside the room's hand-carved walnut doors is a Venetian table. Designer: Mark Nelson, FASID.

Photographers: Dick Sharpe (above)

Harold Davis (below), Max Eckert (opposite)

Garden Views

Extending the indoors to the outdoors and vice versa is as desirable in bedroom planning as it is for any other room in the home. No longer confined to sunny California, such architectural landscaping/decorating combinations abound throughout the country, each presenting its own opportunity to highlight nature at its best the year 'round. Sliding glass doors and large floor-to-ceiling fixed window panels are, of course, the key elements required to make the desired transformation. What's planned and placed on either side is also highly important, for both areas are expected to be private living areas, yet sometimes open to general display. The garden patio may be a walled enclosure, a courtyard common to other rooms in the home, a terrace overlooking a pleasant view or even an enclosed room adjoining the bedroom for purposes of growing plants and flowers the year long. Careful planning eliminates the possibility of tracking plant dirt indoors and minimizes outdoor maintenance. Built-in benches, fountains, planter boxes and the like will increase usability. Outdoor furniture, of course, will let you further enjoy those sunny interludes.

Right: Indoor and outdoor plants are paired on opposite sides of the large sliding glass door in this restful garden bedroom. The massiveness of close-together wood ceiling beams is balanced by the dark, heavy frame of the bed and armoire. The stucco-walled bedroom courtyard has an airiness studded with hanging plants and lightweight wicker furniture. Designer Craig Wright used flagstones for the patio-terrace decking.

Below right: A large, fixed-glass picture window is used in combination with smaller-paned fixed windows to capture a garden patio view. Designer Don Robinson added more glass by means of a floor-to-ceiling mirror that reflects indoor greenery and a painting hung at bedside. A library stand near the charcoal and white draperies holds a dictionary for extra-tough crossword puzzles. The beautiful wood table between lounge chairs holds a few of the owner's collection of carved objects.

Below: Designer Clair Robinson used floor-to-ceiling sliding glass doors for nearly the entire wall of this master bedroom garden patio suite. The two center glass panels slide in opposite directions to open better than 10 feet of space to the out-of-doors. Lush plantings surrounding the colonnaded patio provide privacy and greatly enhance the view. A redwood patio roof between outer wall and house protects the bedroom from unwanted direct sun. The center of the patio area is a swimming pool.

Photographer: Max Eckert (below and top right

Photographer: Dick Sharpe (below)

Photographer: Dick Sharpe (left)

Above: Designer James R. Patterson had the needs of guests in mind when he created this bedroom/study combination. When guests appear, the fold-out bed produces a comfortable setting; when guests aren't around, the room makes an excellent study, complete with music system. Fabric and matching wallcovering, in chevron-dotted tones of spice beige and grass greens, lend a built-in look to the bed wall. The bamboo rod slipped through the bottom of the shade is re-echoed as mitered edging on the shelves.

Opposite: This guest room has an oriental flavor all its own. Designer Virginia Knight used Indian print fabric to cover the twin beds, and picked up their colors in the deep blue walls and cranberry colored carpet. Each bed has its own modernistically styled lamp of shiny brass that extends over the pillows for excellent illumination when reading. Typical of the Far Eastern motif are the decorative accessories — throw pillows, woven baskets, and greenery arrangements.

Guestology

The old cry "Company's coming" needn't cause trauma or put undue anxiety in the mind of today's homemaker. A bit of previous long-term planning and action can make such occurrences exhilarating for guests and hosts alike. And it all begins with having a warm, friendly and comfortable spot to bed down when the day's activities run their tide. For many homemakers, the separate and often cold and characterless guest room has given way to a multipurpose room, gaily splashed with bright colors and patterns and furnished with a sense of fun as well as function. When a guest is not in residence, the room fills an important daily role as a den, sewing area, entertainment center, home office, etc. A comfortable bed is the first prerequisite for a happy guest — and the means of preventing those nagging backaches caused by "sleeping" on a makeshift couch. Convertible sofas, loveseats, and chairbeds are available in a choice of styles and, in the case of the sofa, mattress sizes. Keep in mind that use of lightweight furniture pieces in the immediate area will prevent a moving-man struggle when guests are ready to retire. A trundle bed is another space saver, or you might slipcover a box spring and mattress in colorful fabric to be utilized for seating as well as sleeping. If the guest list numbers several small fry, have some sleeping bags handy.

Guestology

Left: Pattern power on the walls serves to unify the bath and bedroom of this attractive guest suite. While both patterns are informal, they are deliberately color coordinated. One is a calico floral pattern and the other a pert plaid. Furnishings in the bedroom include a gleaming brass bed, a daintily skirted table plus crystal lamp, a fine painting above the bed and an Early American chest to the right of the archway. The bathroom includes a water closet, bathtub with personal shower attachment and built-in vanity with durable plastic laminate countertop. The home's original wood plank bathroom flooring remains highly attractive and blends well with a wicker chair.

Below: Plaid again plays a major role in the decoration of this guest room that often doubles as a sitting area for spur-of-the-moment conversations. The strong chocolate and white pattern dominates the room, yet is softened with the plump pillows and white wall areas. The pillows also are used for seating on the plush amber glow polyester carpeting. Ends of the fold-out bed are crafted of metal to enhance the other unusually decorative metal furnishings which include an occasional table, an ice cream table with chairs and brass boot planters. This bedroom adjoins a fully tiled guest powder room off a center hall. Separate doors make the powder room available from both locations.

Right: Traditional and modern furnishings can make an excellent guest room combination as is seen here. The one-piece plastic chair is much at home with a period-style bed, and a nightstand topped by a spindle lamp with gold and beige shade. The white of the curtains, raised panel door and modern chair provide a nice contrast to the greenish-pink bed quilt, drapes and matching vinyl bathroom wallcovering. The green of the carpeting has been duplicated in feature strips of large tile vinyl floor surfacing in the bathroom and in the toilet seat cover. A large section of wall is surfaced with a door-height mirror illuminated by a theater dressing room fixture. Designer: James Foshey.

Below: A guest room makes a fine retreat for the man of the house and often reflects his special interests via telling accessories. The round-the-world-sailing-enthusiast occupant of this room is also a hunter. His attractive mahogany desk is used for conducting family business and one section of the long wall closet is used for file cabinets, hobby equipment and office supplies. A delicate vinyl print wallcovering has been extended across the ceiling to unify this area with flanking walls, while the other wall surfaces are painted in a cream tone. The chocolate bedspread and chair covering are trimmed in cream, and the sill-depth draperies pick up the brown and cream shadings. Designer: Bill Lane.

Photographer: Max Eckert

Convertible Rooms

The ever-increasing cost of residential living space, be it in home, apartment, condominium or town house, has caused many owners to resort to convertible rooms that can be changed from one use to another at a moment's notice. Such spaces can and should be highly attractive as well as functional. Well-scaled furniture, decorative walls, floors and ceilings, and accessories can be used to establish a mood that is easily shared by the different functions. Bedroom/sitting room combinations often gain the bonus seating space provided by a comfortable daybed. Bedroom/office arrangements can include chaise lounges that needn't betray their after-hours use. Bedroom/sewing room pairings can be highly restful places away from the busier home activities. As is true of any convertible space, the fewer changes required in making the transition from one purpose to another the better. Heavy furniture that must be pushed out of the way in making the switch should be avoided. Chairs should be dual-use, tables should adapt to nightstand duty, and lighting should be sufficient for bedtime reading or full-room illumination.

Neutral and natural, the convertible bed/sofa in this living room is covered in toned and natural stripes, and has arms of natural Philippine rattan. The finish is the same as that of the tables and occasional pieces which were designed by John Mascheroni for style unity. The multi-purpose setting has walls covered with a deep brown paper background with cavorting monkeys in white. The wicker chair blends well with the practical vinyl flooring and gives a high style base to the entire setting.

Photographer: Idaka (above)

Above: Earth tones are good in a man's bedroom, and accomplish an excellent contrast for brass and gold furniture and accessories. In this masculine setting, rich brown fabrics coordinate well with the dark wood parquet flooring, polished leather trunk and vertical desk surfaces. The delicate design of the brass bedstead and etegere help to balance the setting. The antique desk set, complete with feathered quills and a wealth of brass accessories, further beautifies the scene.

Right: A pied-a-terre that doubles as an art gallery — that was the assignment given interior designer Juan Mir by his client. And this is the result! Beige and brown upholstered beds and bolsters were geared to daytime and nighttime duties. The unobtrusive track lighting and white walls were natural choices for picture and sculpture exhibits. Vertical blinds carry the crisp neutrality, floor-to-ceiling, across window walls. And since shade cloth verticals can be rotated 180 degrees, natural lighting is available for art viewing even on the darkest days.

Photographer: Max Eckert (left)

Convertible Rooms

Opposite: Removal of throw pillows and bright satin covers instantly converts this L-shaped sofa into a pair of comfortable beds atop a lavishly decorated wood base that conceals furniture legs. The "Bagdad" sitting/guest room by designer Roger Billingsley moves from a spartan bamboo chair to luxurious ceiling tenting in establishing the Far Eastern decor. The colorfully inlaid table and ancient wood trunk provide repose for artifacts, plants and flowers.

Below: Designer Peg Walker produced a sparkling decor for a teenager who wanted a room to work and entertain in by day, and an extra bed for an occasional overnight guest. One wall is devoted to a delphinium blue and white storage and desk unit, while on the other, a pair of beds set at right angles to each other form a tightly knit conversation group. When needed, one bed pulls out from under the table for sleeping. Multi-width window shades are augmented by a wallpaper mural done in a sketchy black and white.

Photographer: Max Eckert (right)

Convertible Rooms

Left: Decorative wall graphics overlook a single bed built into the corner of this family room. A series of fabric-covered boxes frames the bed, serving as a table and as added seating for the room. The woven appearance of the total area is furthered with rope twist baskets surrounding metal plant containers and the suspended lamp. Stone and wood carvings are contrasted by the large plastic planter bowl and antique tea service. The bed booster and throw pillows generate the color scheme.

Opposite: An open, upper landing in this Southwestern home provided just the space needed for a convertible guest room/ office. Viewed from the bedroom hallway, the area repeats wood beams used in the first-floor decor with the wood railing and ceiling being fully visible from the lower level. One sofa bed slides partially under the corner table when used for seating, while the second bed remains stationary. Designer Charlotte Heuser selected earth-tone fabrics for the bed coverings and cushions.

Below: Interior designers Julie Denison and Ray Kindell, ASID, used a bevy of decorating tricks to produce this unusual sitting/ guest room that spotlights a real backstage dressing table. Wicker storage baskets on wall-mounted shelves are lined with the pistachio velvet of the compact sofa bed, and are trimmed with the turquoise of the paper and chandelier. Ceiling-hung brass chains help to secure the shelves and add a decorative effect. The room-darkening shade was home-trimmed with a blue and green of the trellised paper.

The Attic Lair

One of the most often-remodeled areas of older homes is the attic. Once freed of its usual collection of nearly-discarded "treasures," this space provides an ideal location for children's or parents' activities, especially as a sleeping lair. The open space of an attic is highly conducive to interesting layouts. Beamed ceilings and dormer alcoves add visibly to actual floor space. Wood paneling and decorative wallcoverings quickly transform bare framing into walls and ceilings of great attraction. Various types of lighting fixtures can be used to provide adequate lighting for a variety of activities — or a hole can be cut in the roof for the installation of a skylight to permit daytime brilliance atop the house, away from all activities below. Most conventional attic spaces will provide a 7-foot ceiling height in the center of the room, gradually tapering off to four or five feet at the side walls. This lower space is sufficient for bed and sofa placement and is also excellent space for chests, built-ins and other purposes. Dormer areas often afford an ideal spot for a dressing table or desk, with side walls of the area used for mirrors. Attic spaces being converted to bedroom use should be fully insulated to provide maximum occupant comfort. The open wall and ceiling areas can be quickly fitted with batt insulation before being covered with panel material.

A lot of imagination and basic building materials — wood, acoustical planks and resilient flooring — are the basic ingredients of this handsome attic conversion for a pair of active young boys. Roof support columns help to define the sleep and play areas, while a decorative picket fence covers a large gable window and forms headboards for the beds. The "raft" swing becomes a table when anchored to the floor with chains. The entire room measures 15x27 feet.

Right: Following the traditional attic roof lines, this youthful bedroom takes advantage of every architectural line and puts the entire space to work. The dormer area houses a desk and lamp, end walls provide graceful areas for decorative adjustable shelving, the side wall nestles the brass bed, and the center area of the room provides ample space for occasional and game tables with chairs. One surfacing fabric is used for unification.

Below: The unusual ceiling and wall lines of an attic often can be made a part of the decorative treatment in creating a new bedroom. This home's multi-angle roof resulted in a combination of interior angles blended as one with a decorative plaid wallcovering, which is repeated in the standing screen and bedspread. An area rug is used to define the sitting area of the room which includes a desk-table, dresser, lounge chair and rocker. Accessories range from modern lamps and paintings to an assembly of antique keys. Designer: John Baer, ASID.

Photographer: Idaka (below)

Tight Spot Solutions

Everyone gets into a tight spot once in a while, especially when it comes to finding a little extra space in a home or apartment to accommodate an unexpected overnight guest, or visiting relative. Myriads of ways have been used to solve this problem. Often the solution is a pleasant setting that becomes a daytime seating attraction aside from its primary nighttime function. Tight spot solutions may involve an unused corner in almost any room, or even a closet that can be turned into a compact sleeping nook. Or, maybe a room can be partitioned in such a way to establish still another room. Be sure to keep in mind that furniture makers offer a wide and unique range of beds and other furniture designed to make the best of tight spots.

Opposite: A raised platform surrounded with a permanent wood post-and-beam "canopy" provides both sitting and sleeping space in a most attractive manner. Designer Bruce Stodolla balanced the strength of the white framework with the softness of a pink and white polka dot vinyl wallcovering and mattress covering of the same pattern in a lighter tone. A wicker-and-metal chair blends well with the caramel colored carpeting which covers the entire platform under the mattress. Crystal, gold and white accessories complete the scene.

Below: A generous-size family room provided the answer to finding space for another bedroom in this home. Designer Shindler Pollock selected light and airy latticework and matching bi-fold doors to divide the new area from the family room, yet at the same time make it a part of the family room activity with a built-in storage cabinet incorporating the color television set. When desired, the doors can be folded to reveal just the built-in section, hiding the fact that there is a bed in the area.

Photographer: Max Eckert

Tight Spots

Opposite: Space is where you find it . . . or make it! Here the owner removed a wall separating a summertime sleeping porch, and used the space for year 'round bedroom purposes. The designer, Margot Condon, neatly defined the alcove with wood framing and paneling toned to match the existing bedroom ceiling. Attractive pegged oak flooring was extended into the new space.

This page: One-room apartments challenge the space creativity of all who occupy them, often resulting in "a lot from a little" as this "homemade" corner reflects. The convertible sofa bed and pillows provide daytime seating and comfortable nighttime sleeping. Old fruit packing boxes have been used in their original form to create a staircase storage arrangement for decorative knicknacks, books, and a telephone. Varied cactus plants add shades of green to the setting, which includes a brown-beige-tan wallcovering and brown and white plaid quilt and bed pillow covers. Throw pillows are various shades of brown and gold. An antique trunk doubles as a coffee table during the day and end table at night.

Photographer: Dick Sharpe (left)

Tight Spots

Opposite above: A trio of sofa beds hugs the walls in this compact one-room apartment, providing maximum use of the stem-green colored floor area. The beds serve as seating for small conversational groupings. Circular mirrors create a porthole effect and are reflected in the narrow floor-to-ceiling mirrors adjoining storage cabinets equipped with pull-down fabric doors, also used at right for the corner storage shelves. Designer Peg Walker furnished the room with an easy-to-maintain plastic laminate table.

Opposite below: Three rooms in one may not be possible, but a room that serves three purposes is easy. Virginia Frankel, ASID, designed this combination guest/bedroom as a multi-purpose living center with a common area for sleeping, relaxing and conversation, another for sewing, and a third for make-up and fashion planning. The three vertical floor-to-ceiling divider panels are surfaced with perforated hardboard to provide space for hanging thread, tape measures, scissors, scarves and jewelry.

Below: Floor-to-ceiling sliding pocket doors close off the sleeping area in this compact family room/bedroom combination. The briny motif includes a wealth of nautical accessories, as well as furniture befitting a sea-going pleasure ship. Wood grain ceiling planks combine well with candy-stripe wallcovering and help to balance the weighty appearance of bookcase/desk components. The slide-in, under-bed casework provides still more storage capability, eliminating the need for a bedroom chest of drawers.

Tight Spots

Below: Everything a guest could wish for is provided in a simple but effective way in this small room which has a pleasing mixture of modern lines and charming antiques. The cozy bednook is perkily defined with a provincial print fabric used on walls and as side draperies, as well as for the bedspread. Compact storage on one wall has cabinets, chest and desk in a wall-hung system which also holds plenty of books for nighttime selection. The storage system also incorporates and frames a small window.

Opposite: There's no cause for clutter in this "room for all reasons" designed by Sharon Meadows. Books, serving pieces, objets d'art, bar accoutrements — all find a place in the five-unit modular wall system. Even extra guests have a place — sitting or sleeping in firm comfort on a convertible loveseat that opens to become an 80-inch round bed enfolding the matching ottomans. The abstract forms of the fireplace metal wall sculpture are crafted of steel, copper and brass.

3 For the Young Set

When it comes to planning and decorating a room for the young set, there seems to be no limitation. As the following pages will show, some children go to dreamland each night in a space capsule; others row to sea in search of the "one that got away"; young fire-fighters speed off in engine beds complete with hook and ladders; or they may merely pull over to the side of the road to catch a few winks in a simulated motorcar or authentic antique buggy.

In each instance the setting wouldn't be complete without the supporting cast of "characters," the highly decorative wallcoverings, colorful flooring, purposeful lighting, window-darkening blinds or covers, and the personal accessories that young ones bring home by the pocketful.

Fun-and-fanciful furniture can be a fine incentive to youngsters — even to the point of making their own bed in the morning and picking up their clothes at night. The room can be made a pleasant place in which to play on a rainy day, a quiet spot to do homework, or a retreat.

Color, of course, should be a major ingredient, just as it is in the "go-for-broke" boy's room pictured here. Designer David Landau, ASID, selected a strong and regular pattern carpet to "display" an 11-year-old's unusual bed, an antique buggy totally redone and customized by a cabinetmaker. It may be a child's world, but this young man knows first hand how grandfather enjoyed it!

Sleep Space

The conventional single or double bed is but one of many ways of providing basic sleep space throughout the home, especially when it comes to bunking down youngsters. Built-ins, waterbeds, wall niches, hammocks, sleep-and-sit couches and still other arrangements can be used to supply the basic 39x75" "pad" for a restful night. And with the per-square-foot cost of housing rising all the time, much more consideration is being given to making sleep space perform a daytime function in guest rooms, children's quarters and even the master suite itself. Never before has there been as great a selection of double-duty bed furniture, some of it that appears as much at home in the living room as it does in a traditional four-wall bedroom. The folding bed is an excellent example of the strides that have been made in recent years, to the point that many sofa-beds can't even be distinguished as such; they provide the comfort and appearance of a couch. One-room apartments started the trend to using sofa-beds, but few homes can be found without one sitting ready somewhere. Some homes even have two units, with one of them partially nested into a table-nightstand. Still other popular sleep spaces can be closed off from view when not in use, such as a wardrobe closet combining bed and storage behind attractive wood-carved or louvered doors.

Sleep, storage, study and gameplay are key functions of this high-rise living arrangement for two little ones. Designer Abbey Darer conceived the system which uses two standard 75x30" cot mattresses, a dozen sheets of 4x8' plywood, one flush door, eight wood knobs and vinyl sheet flooring. The finished surfaces of high gloss paint, cotton fabric and vinyl flooring are all washable and wipe-cleanable.

Right: Rock-A-Bye Baby never had it so good! This bedroom for a young girl swings with color and fancy. The swaying, hammock-style bed is suspended from the ceiling with stout nylon marine rope. A seersucker striped bedspread picks up the dominant pink and green colors from the hand-printed floral stripe wallcovering. The sculptured nylon fiber carpet is vibrant golf green. Designer: Virginia Frankel, ASID, Design Associate.

Below: Corners can be made doubly useful with bunk style furniture that's always a hit with youngsters. This lightweight duo is enameled in red, white and blue to carry through the fabric and wallcovering theme. Large slide-out drawers below the lower bunk can be used for clothing or toys. The hinged panel adjoining the ladder drops down to form a desk top supported by rope cords.

Sleep Space

Left: Built-in beds for teenagers can have a flavor all their own. This clean-cut ensemble was quickly and easily constructed with plywood panels to hide an inner box spring and leave just the colorfully-covered mattress visible. The convenient storage case at the foot of the bed doubles as a sturdy bench or game table. An identical pair of cases adjoin the head of the bed for clothes storage. The painted diagonal wall pattern picks up the drawer colors and is repeated in sections of the matching bedspread and window shade.

Below: A very plain bedroom was converted into this attractive teen bedroom and study area. A 3-foot space at one end of the room was used to build an alcove bed/closet combination, leaving the remainder of the room to be used as a study/den. The deep tone of the dark pecan paneling blends with the cool blue-green color scheme of the rest of the room. The flanking closets are equipped with bi-fold doors that slide on overhead tracks to provide full access to contents. A floor cushion serves as a stepping stone to the bed.

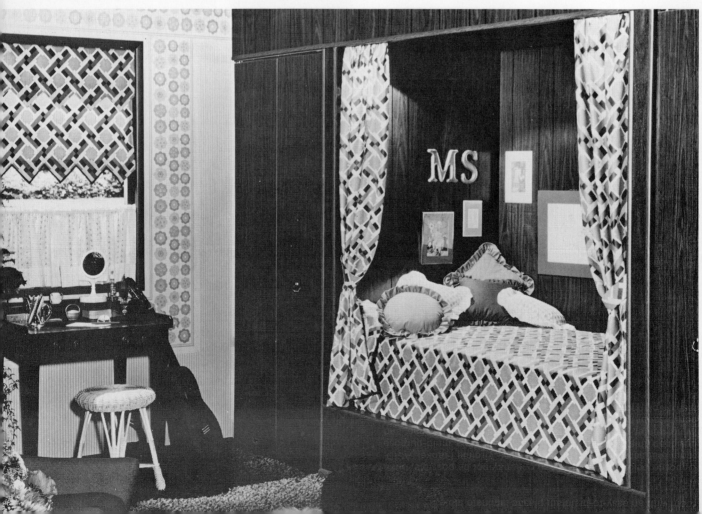

Right: Under-bed storage helps to minimize possible clutter in this bedroom furnished for a teenage boy. The extensive use of wood enhances the manly atmosphere, with the rough-sawn textures highly resistant to scratching. The oak block floor is partially covered by an area rug in the sitting section of the room. One wall of the bed alcove features a diagonal planking which highlights animal horns and a carved totem plaque. The table in the foreground is a large wood burl, highly polished and centered in a metal box planted with a fern.

Below: Boys and bunks are an excellent bedroom solution even when the beds are placed end-to-end instead of in more traditional bunk style. This arrangement maintains maximum empty floor space for playing, while a wall-to-wall bulletin board covered in navy felt handles the everchanging decor. Designer Peggy Walker selected bedspreads in madras print stripe, dark toned for practicality, but brightened by butter-yellow painted walls. The far side of the room holds a double table-desk of butcher block, with natural pine shelves running to the ceiling.

Sleep Space

Left: Built-ins are especially effective in the design and furnishing of a young man's room — they can provide all the needed storage space, desk area and sleeping room without day-to-day movement of furniture. Only the desk chair — and the occupant — move in this room tucked away in an attic space. A large drawer is provided in the bunk base and cabinets are located above the bed at the roof line. The plastic laminate desk top is surrounded by storage cabinets and shelves. Resilient flooring and prefinished paneling helps upkeep remain at a minimum.

Opposite: Sleek and colorful are the structural lines of this modernistic built-in bunk arrangement. Designer Bruce Stodolla extended the form of an art museum pedestal in fabricating the floor-to-ceiling columns which support the upper bunk and the cantilevered bedside shelf. The back wall area of the setting remains open for the ceiling-hung plant. Colorfully patterned, fitted mattress covers include the orange of the bed framework. The carpeting has been extended to form the platform of the lower bunk and coordinates with the wicker armchair.

Below: "Pink at night, sailors delight . . .", but no more of a delight than this on-land quarters for a pair of fun-loving boys. Planned to make the best possible use of all available space, the corner built-in displays the usual collection of "young life" and shares a headboard between the beds. Added toy-and-game storage is provided under the mattress-lid panel of the beds. Cotton sheets were used for bedspread, pillow covering and wall decor. Scrubbable carpeting and deck chairs with removable seat and back canvas simplify clean-up time.

Photographer: Max Eckert (right

Sleep Space

Below: Design students at the University of California at Los Angeles recaptured some of their treasured youthful memories in creating this child's room. The students fondly recalled their enthusiasm for large, colorful graphics, bunk beds, stair climbing, playing with stuffed animals and "just sitting around on a nice soft carpet". The space alloted to this bunk bed is no larger than the usual double-door bedroom closet found in most homes. It was fitted with a built-in chest containing six drawers, with the top surface as the mattress base. The drawers provide ample storage for a youngster's clothing and games, and are on roll-out slides for easy opening and closing. The narrow carpeted stairway at right is the youngster's route to bedtime.

Opposite above: Carole Eichen Interiors designed and custom built these bunk beds to get more mileage from the available area in a bedroom for small children. The beds have tuck-in plaid linen spreads, coordinated with the wallpaper. The extended 36x18" built-in desk surface comes in handy for playtime and classwork assignments with seating provided by a bentwood chair. The twin pin-up lamps have linen shades, again color-coordinated with the bolster and pillows.

Opposite below: A stairway to the stars is this unusual stairway-bunk for youngsters. Built into the corner to conserve valuable play space, the entire unit is carpeted in shag for easy maintenance, without the usual scratches that somehow appear out of the blue. Both lines of the feature stair-step mouldings extend from the painted wall surface to partially conceal built-in lighting. The lower bunk slides into the storage wall when not in use. Designer: Ethel Samuels.

Photographer: Kent Oppenheimer

Photographers: Dick Sharpe (opposite top), Idaka (opposite bottom)

Sleep Space

Right: Nursery sleeping needs have a way of quickly changing as the weeks and months roll by, but this "closet baby" setting can easily be removed for a toddler. Designer Louisa Cowan used floor-to-ceiling screen panels to form the alcove from which there is a natural graduation into the larger room. The bamboo crib is in keeping with other furnishings in the room, and the entire area is carpeted for quiet and comfort. The usual baby clothes tree is used here for a bonnet display.

Opposite: High-ceilinged older rooms make it possible to dramatize the use of large-area space . . . and even use a waterbed! Here a number of modern touches complement the beauty and nostalgia of a young adult's bedroom, complete with stained glass windows and covered cast iron radiator. The low-slung bed frame was fabricated with plastic laminate panels, the horizontal surfaces being usable for headboard accessories and seating. A large ceiling-to-floor hanging lends interest to a wall projection. Designer: Sally Riessen, Chicago, Illinois.

Below: The presence of a dormer in a bedroom offers an unusual challenge with many interesting solutions. This creation by designers Abbey Darer and Bobbi Stuart provides delightful quarters for two young sisters. Pink and white gingham check covers the headboard walls and dramatizes the window-seat bay. Blocks of sun-bonneted girls and farmboys are used pictorially for quilted coverlets and cushions. The vinyl flooring maintains the red and white gambol, with mop-up cleanability.

Photographer: Idaka (left)

Fun & Fantasy

Sleeptime is most important to a young child, but in the minds of many it's equaled by the importance of the surroundings, for it's in the bedroom that the youngster will spend better than half his or her early years. The fun and fantasy of a child's room begins with the sprite imagination and fond recollection of adults, but the finished accomplishment is for all to enjoy. In planning such rooms, every element can be a part of the action, from the fire engine bed to the similar-patterned wallcovering, bedspread and pillows. Or the young man may sail into the horizon on a boat-bed, take a trip to the moon in a space capsule bed or sleep on a Huck Finn raft suspended from the ceiling over a floor of water blue. The windows may provide another spot in which to curl up during daydream time, as fantasies change as often as the weather. Furnishings can be as wild as the imagination. Need a light fixture over a desk? Take a stove pipe, paint it bittersweet, add a whimsical touch by snaking the pipe through a bookcase and have it come out at the desk as a spotlight. Use a fake fur rug for those African safaris, and resilient flooring for a lifesize checker board. Use the walls to provide a painted-on yard stick to measure the occupant's growth. Select put a-way storage units that stimulate the imagination — footlockers, stackable cubes, rearrangeable shelving, built-ins. Choose materials and fabrics that "can take it" and are easily washable. If the room is basically well organized it will hold its own against changing tides, as interests turn from fire engines to bugs or from cut-outs to dolls. A bold and beautiful color scheme can help minimize kid's clutter. Provide as much floor space as possible and keep the setting informal, cheerful and neat. Hopefully, the children will follow suit!

There's nothing subdued about this boy's room, including the boy, we're told! An explosion of color is accented with designs ranging from the brightly stenciled floor to wall full of doodles. A series of chests, high and low, and coordinating desk are used in varying combinations of the room's three main shades: midnight blue, lettuce green and bittersweet. They provide counterspace for all the model ships, gum dispensers and souvenirs collected

Photographer: Kent Oppenheimer (right)

Fun & Fanciful Furniture

Below: The ladder of this red and white fire truck is built into the bunk bed framework to serve double duty — as steps to the top bunk and a support for bookshelves. A removable guard rail simplifies bed-making while swing-down end shelf can be used as a desk or lamp table. Antique-to-modern fire fighting equipment adds to the atmosphere of Engine 51 via coordinated wallcovering, bed covers and pillows. Throw pillows are shaped like familiar signs youngsters soon come to identify and obey. Kneeling on the lower bunk with hat in place, a young fireman has ample windshield through which to visualize his daydreams.

Opposite: Enjoyment of outer space while here on earth was the goal of designer Frank Leo, Color Design Art, in the creation of a child's room in a builder's model home. Extensive use of wood furniture elements exhibits the many possibilities of furnishing secondary bedrooms. The space capsule bed has a 5-foot diameter fitted with red synthetic fur and wet-look vinyl pillows in primary colors. The control center at right is a dresser, while moon and stars are seats for young ones.

Below: "Island Bamboo" sheets rig the mast and a matching blanket covers the deck of the boat-bed to give a girl's room a South Sea Island flavor. The imaginative furniture was designed by the sculptor Accorsi. As a tie-in window treatment, additional sheets frame and edge the white, room-darkening shade. This combination gives it an airy, "fretwork look" that belies its functional quality. The resilient floor and liquid-resistant surfaces of bench and table simplify maintenance.

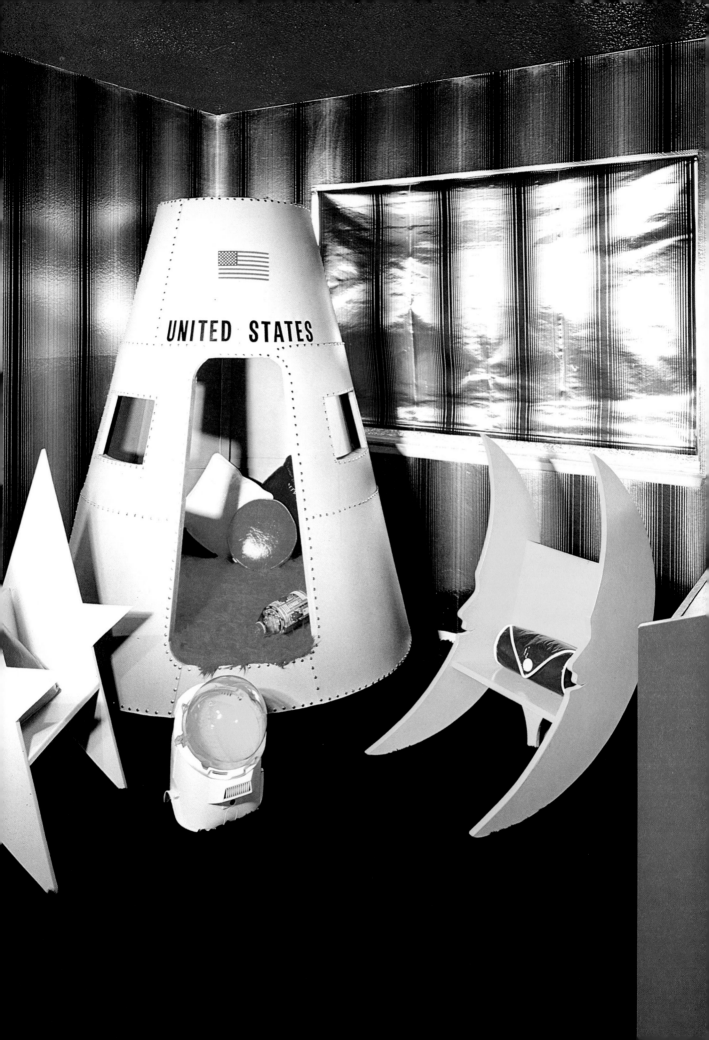

Fun &
Whimsical Walls

Below: Decorator Carole Eichen's passion for fire engines comes through loud and clear in this fun-loving bedroom. Copperwood No. 5 is painted a brilliant red on a beige background, but the fire engine could just as easily have been a wallpaper cut-out. The bed is a standard twin-size mattress and box spring with felt dust ruffle and print coverlet, which, of course, highlights a number of old-time fire-fighting equipment. Still other fire scenes are displayed in book-cover form above the real wood ladder.

Opposite: A little girl's dream come true is this childhood delight. The bed-couch is neatly "fenced in" with pickets, the other side of which are two "playmates" with balloons on high. The quilted bed cover and tiered corner stand provide a daytime home for this moppet's expansive doll collection. Play furniture in wicker and maple provide a pleasing scale in appearance, in addition to being highly functional. The large sliding glass doors are framed with a ruffle and floor-to-ceiling shutter panels. Designer: Carole Eichen.

Photographers: George Szanik (below), Dick Sharpe (right)

Fun &
Window Wonders

Opposite: The typical tract home aluminum bedroom window takes on a new appearance and becomes the delight of youngsters in this compact setting. A simple plywood panel cut-out was painted vivid colors and nailed to the wall for an unusual window frame. Bright red balls help to separate the carved panel from a larger surround, making space for pull-down shade. The mattress of the corner built-in lifts to provide storage for playthings. Designer: Hamilton-Howe.

Below: A large circular window gave inspiration to this Raggedy Ann n' Andy child's bedroom/playroom combination. Located less than two feet from the floor, the window height permits youngsters to easily view the out-of-doors while enjoying a tete-a-tete over cookies and milk. Cardboard cut-outs of storybook characters balance the paper rule, which is used to measure the heights of the fast growing children. The Raggedy Ann carpeting is soil-hiding nylon, sturdy enough to handle heavy traffic.

Photographer: Max Eckert (left)

Put-a-way Planning

Put-a-way planning in the bedroom should begin with the careful selection of furniture that can pick up where closet space leaves off. It's a rare room that is enhanced in appearance by clutter, and this is especially true when it comes to children's bedrooms. A bedside table is standard in most bedrooms and with its shelves and drawers can provide at-hand storage. Headboards frequently have compartments, either open or concealed, as well as shelf space for reading lamps, decorative accessories and the like. Additional shelving is easy to install with screw-to-the-wall standards and adjustable shelf supports available at most all building materials outlets. These units can be used with wood, plastic or glass shelving and can be an integral part of the room's decorative scheme. On-the-wall storage systems also can incorporate compact furniture which makes the bedroom more functional. Some units have drop-down desks, and compartments for a sewing machine, television, stereo and other items. The basic bedroom closet itself often may be expanded to occupy an entire wall, with floor-to-ceiling doors, for maximum utilization of interior space. This space can best be utilized by wise planning.

Above: Children's room storage for toys and games is most efficient when open shelves are used instead of a closet or series of drawers. Youngsters can quickly locate what they're seeking without pawing through or climbing over a dozen other objects that tend to end up in a heap. These window-flanking shelves are fixed in place, as is the window-sill shelf unit. The settee was converted from a baby crib. Clothes are stored in drawers below the bed.

Opposite: Adjustable storage units and shelves permit easy rearrangement in a child's bedroom. As the youngster grows from grammar school through high school or college, desks, cabinets and shelves can be placed at the desired level on wall rails. This wall, designed by Albert Herbert, ASID, has twin drop-front desks, sliding door cabinets, glass-fronted units, several sizes of shelves and drop-front woven wood storage cabinets.

Put-a-way Planning

Opposite above: Everything "works" in this young man's bed-room/study by designer Peg Walker. Wallcoverings artfully define clutter-concealing, slim built-in cupboards which, in turn, frame a many-drawered slab-desk and create an "open end" division of study and sleeping areas. And everything is planned for wipe-clean treatment to maintain a "new" look. The window shade treatment highlights Peruvian stripes in random tones of Andes blue and bright lime, cooled by crisp white. Sheets and pillow cases add to the striped effect. The great amount of cabinet and drawer space keeps clutter to a minimum.

Opposite below: Incentive for tidiness on the part of a young boy is prompted by this wall storage system arranged by Albert Herbert, ASID. It provides all the stuff-away and show-off space a boy could want — plenty of shelf space for books and mementos, cabinets with roomy drawers for clothes, and desk units for homework and hobbies. The off-the-floor units simplify floor cleaning and permit background wall areas to be decorated in a variety of ways. Each component in the system can be moved around as needs over the years. This wall unit is available in walnut, teak or oak.

Below: The storage "ell" of this nursery is intended to meet changing needs as the baby crib is supplanted by a junior bed. Without taking up much room, the corner cabinet arrangement contributes an enormous amount of shelf and storage space and later can become a commodious desk and dresser. Interior de-signer Carl Fuchs has used coordinated stripe fabric-laminated shades at the windows, and the same striped fabric as facing for the built-in cabinets, and on the bias as a change of pace for the draft-protecting screen. The primary colors involved are yellow, tangerine and mocha.

Put-a-way Planning

The happy world of Dr. Seuss inspired this arrangement of colorful, modern and practical furnishings and accessories. Storage cubes are painted Bloopy blue, Overly orange, Yertle yellow, Grinch green and Quite white, all colors particularly appealing to children. The cubes can be rearranged at will to be used in the center of the room for seats and game time. Striped wallpaper creates a tented ceiling effect, and the rug especially designed for this room is reminiscent of a circus ring.

Hide-away storage in the room has been increased by the use of the closet door for still more storage boxes in the popular colors. Lower walls of the closet are surfaced with perforated hardboard for hanging the dozens of odd-shaped items that find their way into a boy's lair. Original drawings by and from Dr. Seuss himself were loaned from his private collection for display in this room designed by Jody Greenwald. The post at right frames the trundle bed, which is another space-saver.

Photographer: Harold Davis

A simple store-bought rope ladder provides unique put-a-way space in this bedroom for scarves, belts, chains, necklaces and other "long" items that add to the decor. The ladder is suspended from the ceiling by means of two decorative hooks and ends approximately two feet from the floor. Interior designer Cynthia Silverstein used a much larger child's swing in the living room of this home to provide additional seating area. Walls and ceiling of the bedroom are papered in inexpensive gingham. The wood floor has two small area rugs and both the foot and headboard of the bed are made of picket fence painted white.

Interesting and effective put-away space often can be achieved on even a limited budget. Designer Toni Lenhart came up with an unusual solution here with the help of her local milk dairy. Each of the wall-hung wire baskets is really an old milk rack spray painted and secured to the wall with inexpensive clips. Some of the baskets are used horizontally and others vertically to create the attractive area for stuffed animals, plants and bric-a-brac. The walls are covered with 79¢-a-roll wallpaper which came pre-pasted for fast application. Curtains are inexpensive cotton trimmed with ribbon and hung on a cafe rod.

Put-a-way Planning

A perfect set-up for Cub Scouts and Little Leaguers, this snappy red, white and blue bedroom is comprised of a bed, chest/ wardrobe, desk, bookcase hutch, ladder, mirror, bulletin board and guard rail, all assembled to attract any youngster. The wardrobe units include adjustable rails for placement of shelves at desired heights. The brass hardware is in vivid contrast to the brilliant red. Room accessories include a prefabricated steel circular stairway that's great for aspiring yachtsmen. Roll-up window shades are in keeping with basic room colors.

Right: The building block idea is put to good use in a child's room with a system of panels and connectors which can be built up into any arrangement needed. The white lacquer finish on the wood panels is scratchproof. Devised in Denmark, this component system includes three sizes of panels, a base unit and colored sliding doors that make it possible to construct shelving and cabinet storage of any size and arrangement.

Below: Conservation of space and maximum utilization of same was accomplished with this built-in bed/dresser/bookcase/storage unit fabricated from plywood panels. The dual-level unit incorporates a standard-size single bed mattress above an arrangement of nine drawers of varying width and height dimensions. A table lamp is used at the head end of the bed while a smaller, directional reading lamp is placed at the other end. The far end can be used as a desk top while sitting on a floor pillow. Recessed cubicles in the vertical surface panels provide storage for clock, books and small-fry treasures. The wall is made more interesting with a graphic arrow.

Put-a-way Planning

Right: Modular storage components add considerably to the efficiency of this bedroom providing an appropriate place and space for both essentials and decorative items. The recessed wall units have swing-down panels, one of which is used for a desk and the other as a make-up table. Pigeonholes prove handy for desk accessories, letters, cards and the like. Storage shelves above the closing sections are adjustable, as are those in the headboard. The bed itself is adjustable to several heights for reading and relaxing. All surfaces of the bed unit and storage wall cases are durable plastic laminate that is easily maintained.

Below: Storage modules available from a number of manufacturers permit total flexibility in designing drawer and cabinet space for active youngsters. This setting for a younger tot employs thirteen boxes, four of which have totally open interiors and the balance with two divider panels which accept drawers, or may be used for either horizontal or vertical storage. The thin wood cubes may be stacked to desired height, even arranged in a semicircle if preferred. Aside from providing storage for a young child, the components add to play-time enjoyment and the drawers can be used for moving smaller items from the room.

Photographer: Elyse Lewin
Designer: Cheryl Lewin

Left: Do you like to show off those prized possessions you've collected over the years? What better place than in your own bedroom? There are a variety of ways to solve the problem of bedroom shelving and display space, and shown here is a low budget and attractive solution. This teenage girl's bedroom wall was blank until it was fitted with wood soda pop cases obtained from a local beverage store. The units are simply stacked one atop another and may be moved at a moment's notice. They also come in handy when it comes time to move and you need something in which to pack all those treasured items.

Below: Built-in storage can be a key design element in a bedroom as is the case in this young lady's room designed by Charlotte Heuser. Floor-to-ceiling cabinets line the better part of two walls providing spaces that will easily meet new demands as the youngster grows. The built-in desk is in front of a window overlooking the yard and the near-by hardboard display panel will eventually become a drawing table, with space below for a stool. The myriad of cubbyholes surrounding the display board is balanced by the openness of the opposite wall which features movable shelves and two large lower cabinets with doors.

Photographer: Max Eckert

4 Decorating

Decorating or redecorating a bedroom can be fun and exciting. The result, of course, should be a deep visual pleasure to be enjoyed anytime of the day or evening, with just the right lighting, stereo or television switch within fingertip reach, a squishy chaise for relaxing, and a bed to refresh the weary body at the end of an eventful day.

Undertaking such a project needn't involve outside help, but it's there in abundance if you need it. Likewise, it needn't deplete your bank account if you shop wisely, plan smartly, and execute many of the details within the talents of most reasonably enterprising owners.

If you're a romanticist saddled with strictly utilitarian bedroom furniture, you'll love what a toile wallcovering with matching fabric will do. Let the pattern climb every wall, even the slanted dormer type, and use the fabric lavishly for window treatments, bedspread, pillows, table covers. The result will be a romantic softness. A nostalgic floral design in your favorite colors would be another good choice.

Creating a country-fresh mood is the easiest challenge of all. Go with a sweet calico design, a fresh gingham, a smiling floral, or the crafty patchwork look. It's a good idea to cover the ceiling as well as the walls if you don't have much furniture. Eyelet ruffled pillows, bed linens and curtains are great for this look. So are baskets for needlework in progress, your favorite magazines or dried grasses and flowers. Or try the natural look — wonderfully serene and therefore perfect for the private retreat.

Photographer: Max Eckert

Decorating

Serenity is an integral part of the Oriental decor. A mural with delicate flowering branches will set the stage beautifully. The lacquered nesting tables, shoji screens, and gingerjar lamps can be added as the budget allows. Or, if you love Victoriana, a smile of artful pattern in exciting colors is the ticket. But don't stop with the walls. Continue the pattern power wherever fabrics can be used. A dramatic pattern of this sort is also great for routing architectural obsolescence from any room. Old porch wicker furniture, lacquered white and treated to cushions covered to match the walls, will do as much for a Victorian room as a costly Tiffany lamp. Potted palms suit this decor, too.

Wall murals with "views" of Venetian palazzos, Grecian temples, and Cote d'Azure are fabulous for those with yacht tastes and rowboat budgets. Murals also help "furnish" a room, and they are eye-

Irregular wall and ceiling surfaces afford the opportunity to use contrasting yet compatible colors to highlight the shapes. Designer Raul Coronel selected brown and gold for this setting which is reflected in large mirror closet doors.

Photographer: Dick Sharpe

savers in no-view situations. Love the outdoors? Then you'll love wall designs that turn your room into a forest, a meadow, a vine-covered gazebo. Complete the look with reed blinds, lots of real greenery and rattan furniture.

Whatever your decor, choose colors you truly love, but be prepared to let the proportions and location of the bedroom dictate in what dosages they should be used. A chilly room facing north would hardly benefit from a large expanse of ice blue, for example. But if the ice blue shows up as an accent in an essentially warm-hued wallcovering — say, a peach-colored floral — everything would be fine and dandy. By the same token, you'd find an all-orange room tough to live with in a hot climate. But when contrasted with lots of white the orange will be tangy rather than hot. Finally, keep in mind that you are the person who should be most pleased.

Mexican elements set the pace for this bedroom designed by Snyder-Brunet & Cie. The walls and ceiling are heavily-troweled plaster with yucca poles set into holes carved out of the material. The heavy linen bedspread is hand embroidered.

Photographer: Elyse Lewin

Creative Headboards

Creative headboards often begin with a plain wall and end up as the main attraction in a delightful bedroom. The style, shape, material or fabric selected provide the means with which to extend an idea, a theme or a desire. Headboards, of course, needn't be a part of the bed itself regardless of the material involved — even a brass bedstead can be secured to the wall. And the headboard can be an important part of the storage, with concealed compartments that eliminate the need for nightstands or a bedside table. Lights, lighting controls and other electronics for drapery control, television, stereo, can be incorporated into the headboard.

Entertainer Sally Struthers found a fanciful three-panel screen at a Southern California auction and purchased a bed quilt in Hawaii. The two were given to Jay Steffy who made them the center of attraction for Miss Struther's bedroom. The floral panels are set at an angle in a 90-degree corner of the room, and are built into a headboard/shelf/nightstand setting, all of which conceal an undesirable corner window. Throw pillows and shelf accessories add further interest.

Right: Two colors of velvet were applied to plywood in the fabrication of the wall-mounted headboard for this custom waterbed. The framework incorporates pillow supports that prevent push-down in the water. The bedside shelving eliminates the need for nightstands, and supports the metal band equipped with three light globes. Phoebe Common, Associate ASID, designed the room with various mountain and desert elements such as carpeting in four colors, shaped like mountains. Deep purple velvet was appliqued horizontally for the bedcover.

Below: Interior designer Marco Wolff, Jr., selected an 18th Century Boiserie headboard to establish the focal point of this bedroom. The graceful wood carving is affixed to the vinyl-covered wall, apart from the king-sized bed which has a quilted silk spread. Toile nightstands have a pewter finish and support antique Chinese vase lamps with pleated silk shades. The bed throw is Hyrax fur from Argentina. The lucite-bronze-glass dressing table displays a Russian jeweled box.

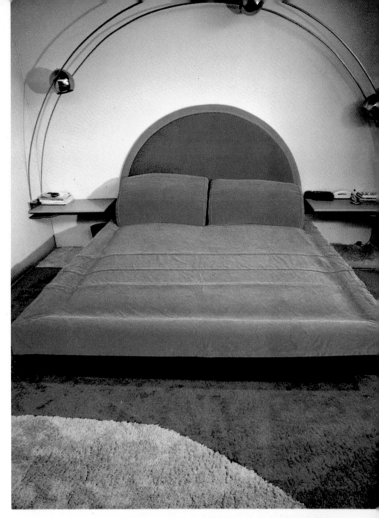

Photographers: Richard Fish (above), Max Eckert (below)

Photographer: Glen Allison
Designer: Alexander Girard

Creative Headboards

Left: Oriental orange, dark wood tones and gold door framing compose the total color scheme of this master suite, aside from the milk-white bedside lamps. The entire headboard wall is finished in mirror with wood slats radiating outward to form a rising sun pattern. The carpeting, which matches the quilted bedspread in color, rises up the mirrored wall helping to form a platform for the built-in nightstands which in actuality are long, one-drawer-high platforms.

Opposite: As colorful as it is creative, this bedroom wall serves both as a headboard and a showcase for a unique collection of dolls from around the world. The figurines are shown to best advantage by lighting fixtures hidden within the wall, while the room itself is amply illuminated by natural lighting from the glass wall and large skylight. Brightly hued patchwork bed cover, pillows and drapes are set off handsomely by the pure white of the walls and woodwork. Stereo is in easy reach located in bedside cabinet.

Below: Decorative latticework panels are used throughout this bedroom to create the unusual headboard, nightstand niches, dresser recess and furniture fronts. Painted bone white, the latticework produces an excellent framework for walls painted midnight blue or papered with a blue-green pattern on white. The carpeting is grass green, matching the leaves of the bedcover design. Still more green is introduced by tabletop and floor plants spotted around this room designed by Dennis Banchoff.

Photographers: Kent Oppenheimer (above), Max Eckert (below

Fabric Phenomenon

The occupant of a bedroom determines to a large extent the fabrics selected for use in the room. Basically, they are all good, but some are better for specific situations, such as using washable cottons for a child's room instead of fine silk that would not take the day-to-day action. A good test to follow in choosing a bedroom fabric is to crumple a small piece of the material in your hand. If it wrinkles, it's either too thin or too perishable and will require more-than-normal maintenance. Linens and laces can provide a beautiful appearance, but if they are too thin, you'll be faced with constant wrinkling problems. Many decorators and homeowners rely heavily on treated fabrics that will extend wear without sacrificing appearance. Professionally treated with a plasticizing agent, a bedspread or other bedroom fabric becomes washable and has a "cellophane-like" surface protection against soiling. Flammability is another consideration in selecting bedroom fabrics. Some materials, like fiberglass, have this inherent quality, while other materials can be treated to provide the safety feature. Both dacron and fiberglass are widely used for upholstering wall areas and custom headboards.

Above: An undulating print fabric sweeps across the walls, and everything in this room seems to flow with it. The double bed, under a layer of stylized flowers and geometric pillows, drifts along, lit on either side by the ethereal touch of two hanging lamps. The furniture, in pure white with touches of chrome, provides a solid contrast to the surrounding deep colors. Angular fretwork pattern of the headboard repeats in the dresser front.

Opposite: Colorful silk fabrics further define the slightly recessed headboard area of this dramatic master bedroom setting created by designer Robert Hutchinson. The overriding gold of fabric and carpeting is contrasted by charcoal colored fabrics and lighter tones of an occasional table and cushioned wicker armchair. The white panels in the draperies and pillows blend the major colors.

Photographer: Max Eckert (right)

Fabric Phenomenon

Below: Designer Douglas Sackfield began the creation of this bedroom with a marvelous cotton print, a bright poppy on beige and white geometric ground. He covered the bed with the material and repeated the same fabric as pillow shams, table skirt and wallpaper. Just the poppy on white was used for curtains and ruffles for the four poster bed, and a random stencil repeats the flower on the floor. The armoire, bed, desk and chair are all wood-crafted authentic reproductions of 18th century French-Canadian furnishings. Bone white accessories complete this setting.

Right: Black-and-white cotton was uphol-stered to a fiberglass backing for the walls and decorative center ceiling beam of this room designed by Joan Stevens. The antique brass and polished steel bed has an underdrape and cover of Belgian lace topped by a beautiful Oriental runner and period tapestry pillows. The backless antique setee has white satin cushions and a needlepoint pillow. The large Ori-ental scroll above the bed is flanked by an Oriental carved wood plaque with ivory figures. Cotton fabric was also used for the drapes and tiebacks, and as a circular table drape.

Below: The Wonderful World of Sheets continues to expand daily in the decora-tive treatment of bedrooms. This arrange-ment by designer Philip Campbell uses nothing but sheets for all fabric applica-tions. The daybeds in red-and-white and green-and-white stripes are fitted by means of decorative rosettes at each end. Sack-style pillows duplicate the end tie of the bedsheets. Solid-color sheeting sewn together with ragged edges provides an interesting wall decoration. The warmth of oak flooring is enhanced by an area rug between the beds, furnishings, and decorative plants and flowers.

Photographers: Dick Sharpe (above), Elyse Lewin (below)

Fabric Phenomenon

Below: Batik, a "busy design" pattern printed in Indonesia with a wax process that is very popular in the Orient, is employed throughout this distinctive bedroom for bed cover, pillows, chair cushions, lamp shades, and tablecloth. The red and white fabric selected by Eileen Kreiss of Kreiss Imports repeats a leaf pattern. Bamboo shades are used in abundance as wallcoverings and as an overhead to create an interesting affect for an otherwise dull ceiling. Sisal matting is used as a floor covering as well as for a covering for one of the walls. Potted palm adds to the flavor.

Opposite: Three screen-printed fabrics and two matching vinyl wallcoverings were combined in the design of this elegant bedroom. The decorative border of the paisley design provides an excellent frame for the bed, wall sections and windows. The small Indonesian arrowhead design fabric used for the table top repeats in the foot stool. A chandelier light fixture provides necessary illumination at the table while a bedside lamp gives further three-level light. A white fur area rug contrasts well with dark wood flooring, which is further contrasted by white moulding and trim.

Photographer: Elyse Lewin (below)

5 Elegant Bed Ideas

The living room may be the showcase of a home, but the bedroom reveals the owner's tastes in subtle ways — starting with the bed itself. Through history the bed has been a keynote of decoration. Wealthy ancients encrusted their beds with jewels. Later Europeans counted on the bigness of the bed and the richness of its trappings to show that they had arrived. Fashionable ladies received guests in the bedroom until the mid 19th century. Their horizontal drawing-rooms were designed to knock the eyes out of their friends.

The bed is just as important today. Topping the scale are the custom-made types — circular or unique king size beds that are one of a kind, offering styling that immediately captures the beholder's fancy. Four-poster styles are much in vogue regardless of the period styling selected for the bedroom, from modern to Victorian. Headboards are often upholstered in rich, delicate fabrics — or formed of wood carvings, Oriental wall hangings, or shining metals.

Bed elegance can be achieved in many ways, as the art deco bedroom at left indicates. Textures can be mixed, from velvet to chrome. Tree trunks and limbs can be combined for a natural setting. Fabric canopies can range from traditional to modern, from solid wood ceilings to mirrored surfaces to frilly lace. Bed curtains can be used to complete the setting, or the popular brass bed can stand on its own to give a gleaming decor.

Elegant Bed Ideas

Contemporary Canopies

Opposite: Gleaming metal furniture has long been used in living rooms to provide a shining elegance to the modern home. Today, the material is fast making its mark in the bedroom, where its polished appearance sets the theme around which entire room settings revolve. Here, polished aluminum is used in simple splendor to reflect color and pattern. The gleaming base of the queen-sized four-poster bed gives an added dimension to the oriental rug. The corner etagere and lower table have brass inlays to add a warm glow to polished aluminum. The tailored and trim furniture lines are relieved by the abstract sculptural form of the metal mirror, the fluid figures in the stone rubbing, and by the shapely accessories. Walls are finished in a light color to contrast with a dark flooring.

Below left: Wood and fabric are the key components of this contemporary canopy bed, designed for do-it-yourself construction. The upright and cross poles are 1¼ inch in diameter, and support three strips of 11-inch wide fabric, each 7 yards in length. The wood base frame has a cross member and four corner blocks for supporting the box spring and mattress. Navy, red and yellow pillows add color.

Below: Designer Milo Baughman selected honey tone olive ash burl for the posts, canopy frame and surround of this contemporary bed. The same material was used in the manufacture of the nightstand and a double wardrobe not visible here. A pair of ottomans stand at the foot of the bed and are upholstered in a contemporary patterned fabric to enhance the modernistic styling of the bedroom.

Elegant Bed Ideas

Classic Canopies

Left: The influence of Thomas Chippendale's early Georgian furniture design continues today as American firms supply popular 18th Century styling for bedrooms. Prior to Chippendale, most four-posters were swathed in draperies, with little wood showing through. His designs placed emphasis on the beauty of posts ornamented by carvings and finials. This bed in oak veneer reflects the period's elegance.

Opposite: Fit for a king and appropriately named the King Henry VIII, this four-poster boasts beautifully turned columns, gold-leafed feet and mirrored ceiling and headboard. A creation of Phyllis Morris Originals, the bed is fitted with crewel curtains and cover, matching the upholstered wall. The Consulate nightstands have St. Regis candelabras. A Persian carpet is centered in the room.

Below: True to tradition, this spacious four-poster bed is based on an original 18th century design. Its gracefully turned posts, featuring brass ornamentation, rise to delicate finials on top. The headboard shows the simplest of shaping, setting off the posts on either side.

Photographer: Kent Oppenheimer (right)

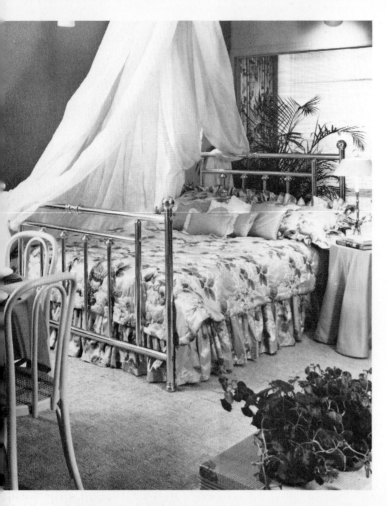

Elegant Bed Ideas

Bold & Brass

Left: The brass bed has always reflected a special elegance, as well as sparked many a decorators' imagination for unusual surroundings. As the center piece of this tropical bedroom, the brass bed has a quilted coverlet and dust ruffle beneath a romantic mosquito netting. Track lighting fixtures can be relocated at will to spotlight the natural foliage.

Opposite: A do-it-yourself canopy helps to make a brass bed the center of attention in this master bedroom, designed to be a summertime haven for warm weather fans throughout the year. The leafy green and white print is repeated on the chair and ottoman, while the white of the fabric is used for walls and the gold in furnishings and accessories.

Below: Fluffy white carpeting plus dark painted and paneled walls were selected to maximize the gleaming appearance of this four-poster style brass bed. The decorative scrolls, as well as the vertical members of the bed, create their own design elements and are complemented by a patchwork quilt cover that gives the room its only pattern. The bedside table also is brass with a glass top.

6 Planning Aids

Planning is the key when it comes time to bring the best of your ideas to fruition. And the more source information you accumulate for your planning sessions, the better armed you become to get the job done quickly and efficiently.

The best sources of information on any product, of course, are the product manufacturers themselves. Aware of this fact, most manufacturers now offer informative and visually exciting literature packages to the homeowner to help him during this very important planning stage.

Don't be afraid of the manufacturer's literature because you think it may be unfairly biased, or just a lot of inflated ad copy — most of it is honest, straightforward and filled with valuable and helpful facts. Of course, knowing what to look for in the way of useful information will help you get the most out of whatever literature you receive. The biggest booklet or the prettiest pictures don't always convey the most information — sometimes they do, but quite often a single sheet can give you as much useful data as you need to begin your remodeling or building project.

As you look through the literature previews on the next pages, consider your needs: Are you looking for ideas, or hard product information? Both are readily available, often in the same package. When you've made your decision, simply turn to the index on page 124 and 125 and send your request to the manufacturers.

Planning Aids

HISTORIC DECORATING. For tastes that favor authentic colonial designs, the Craft House offers a handsome book of Williamsburg Reproductions. Chapters give information on the Colonial Williamsburg Foundation's restoration efforts and on fabrics, furniture and wallcoverings used in homes of the era. These background pages are complemented by color photography of Williamsburg room settings. Price is $5. Craft House.

SWEDISH SURPRISE. Convenient is the Swedish-style trundle bed that rolls out, then swings up easily to match heights with top bed for use separately or together as a unit. A variety of platform beds constructed with resilient wooden steam-bent slats lets you enjoy back support without that bedboard feeling. Also available are sofas, wall systems and a multitude of chair styles. Price of catalog is $1. Door Store.

PAPER DOLLS FOR ADULTS. The Furniture Fitter lets you visualize how new furniture will look in your home before you buy. To use, cut out the template for the furnishing you like and check the dimensions printed on the bottom (say, 46" wide). Take two small objects and place them 46" apart on the floor, next to the wall; close one eye, and move the piece until it fits into the space between the two objects. The cut-apart catalog offers a collection of popular furniture designs. Price is $2. American-Drew.

ROMANTIC TRADITION. Aromatic, cedar-lined Love Chests are spacious, air-tight, and built to last. They range in style from Deacon's Bench to Mozambique, in finish from red enamel to weathered Tulipwood, in accent from antique brass to vinyl upholstery. A packet of brochures on chests and more is 50¢. Lane.

CUSTOM BRASS DESIGN. Extruded solid brass is used in the construction of custom headboards, beds and such elegant accessories as standing coat hangers and cheval mirrors. A diverse selection of bed designs is shown in a vibrant color catalog — straight, simple lines, ornate scrollwork, offbeat curves, or soaring canopies. The price is $3. Bedlam Brass Beds.

Comfortably scaled to the smaller bedroom, this hutch bed features the leaded glass look with amber inserts. The armoire measures only 38" wide by 78" high, yet boasts three trays and four shelves behind its double doors. These oak pieces belong to the Main Street USA collection. Bassett.

Cado

BUYING A MATTRESS. "How to Buy a Mattress" is a booklet designed to help you make a wise and knowledgeable choice when purchasing a mattress. The booklet includes facts on different mattress constructions and mattress care. Price is 25¢. Simmons.

The Ello Bunch, a modular arrangement of bedroom furniture, is made of white polyester laminate which is both durable and easy to clean. The doors are offered with a washable suede front, in ash burl or with a natural cane front.

FLEXIBLE MODULES. Endless design possibilities with flexible Cubex modules are presented in an informative color brochure. Each Cubex module consists of three wooden rectangles and a base which can be tapped gently together by hand with the use of black connectors. From this simple starting point, you can build up, combine and supplement endlessly to keep in tempo with changing needs. Cado.

BEDDING BOOKLET. The maker of Perfect Sleep mattresses and foundations has dedicated this 14-page "Bedroom Book" to anyone planning a first bedroom. The entertaining booklet contains a brief history of the bed, discusses the proper selection of bedding, and shows how to do exercises in bed. Also, how-to tips for functional furniture arrangement. Price is 75¢. Serta.

Engraved Italian burl print is presented in this contemporary wall storage system. The 76" high components include display, desk and TV units, all measuring 36" high. All have a combination of glass and solid doors, drawers and removable shelves, and interior illumination. Schoolfield Furniture.

Please refer to index on page 124 and 125 for manufacturers' addresses.

Planning Aids

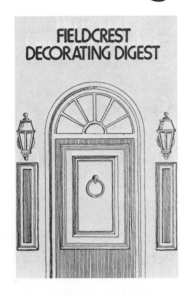

HOW-TO WITH SHEETS. A 60-page "Decorating Digest" that offers innovative ideas using sheets, towels, bedspreads, and blankets for economical decorative effects. Includes patterns and instructions for making everything from plantstands to dust ruffles to roller shades. There are seventeen projects in all. Price is $1. Fieldcrest.

GETTING BEAUTY AND VALUE FOR YOUR DECORATING DOLLARS. A fully illustrated 96-page guide that covers the basics of decorating and provides tips on shopping for furniture and home furnishings. Includes a glossary and shows examples of various decorating themes such as American Traditional, Colonial, French Provincial, Contemporary and Mediterranean. Price is 50¢. Ethan Allen.

UPHOLSTERED FURNITURE. Information on how to care for your upholstered furniture is covered in a 20-page booklet that includes directions for routine care, suggestions for removing stains and cleaning methods. Price is 50¢. National Association of Furniture Manufacturers.

ANTIQUE DESIGNS. Offered in a 31-page catalog are hand-tied bed canopies, all authentic copies of antique designs. Also available are quilts, coverlets, curtains, rugs and handmade furniture. Laura Copenhaver.

Laura Copenhaver Industries

FOR FURNITURE SHOPPERS. To help furniture shoppers help themselves, the "Truth in Shopping" booklet shows you how to avoid future complaints by knowing how to shop wisely. How to select a furniture fabric is discussed in "The Cover Story," telling you everything you need to know to select the correct upholstered fabric for your budget and lifestyle. Price of each is 25¢. Kroehler.

DECORATING DATA. A convenient pocket-size home decorating and planning kit in folder form contains planner cards, individually tabbed and coded with all the information one needs to know about each room in the house. A pouch for paint chips, fabric, carpet and wallpaper samples makes up the other sections of the folder. Price is $1.75. Decorating Data.

MODERN DECORATING GUIDE. Hundreds of ideas on decorating are presented in this practical handbook written by three experts in the field of contemporary interior decorating. Lavishly illustrated with color room scenes plus many black-and-white photographs, the guide includes shopping tips and room planning information to help you buy without making mistakes. Price is $2. Founders.

CREATIVE HOME PLANNING GUIDE. This booklet is full of simple ideas to help you make your house a "home." Arrangement of space (floor plans, traffic patterns) and systems you can build into your home for your family's convenience are applied to specific areas in the home. A companion booklet entitled "Home Security Guide" provides fire and security protection information along with helpful tips. Price is $1. NuTone.

AMERICANA COLLECTION. Early American reproductions and handcrafted originals, including decorative accessories for the entire house, are presented in a colorful 80-page catalog. Among the 20,000 items offered are clocks, lamps, light fixtures, baskets and pottery, woodenware, rugs, stoves, wall hangings, furniture and documentary fabrics and wallcoverings. Jenifer House.

FINE ART POSTERS. An extensive selection of limited edition fine art posters is presented in a handy folder-type catalog. In full color and black and white, the posters can be framed or hung as-is to provide decorative accents. Price is $2.50. Poster Plus.

COUNTRY TOUCH. Ruffles, fringe and delicate fabrics are combined to make curtains that have a traditional country air. Bed and canopy ensembles are also presented in a 39-page catalog, as is a special collection of Waverly fabrics suitable for slipcovers, bedspreads and draperies. Country Curtains.

SOURCES FOR AUTHENTIC OLD-HOUSE PRODUCTS. The Old-House Journal Buyers' Guide is a unique catalog that tells where to buy authentic products for restoring and decorating houses built before 1914. More than 300 specialty companies are listed. Price is $5.50. The Old-House Journal.

MIRROR IDEAS. "Mirror Magic" is a photographic tour of 21 leading model homes and apartments that show you how to put mirrors to work for you. There are 68 mirrored room settings and 21 floor plans, with location mirrors indicated, showing how mirrors relate to both the specific and adjacent rooms. Price is $1. National Assn. of Mirror Mfrs.

Please refer to index on page 124 and 125 for manufacturers' addresses.

Planning Aids

CARPET MAINTENANCE — An 8-page carpet care guide explains how to treat specific stains and gives helpful maintenance hints. It also includes information on various carpet performance characteristics. Armstrong.

HARDWOOD FLOORS. 20 pages of exquisite flooring in both wide and narrow planks, squares and mosaic parquet. Shows room scenes with a visual variety of color, style and texture in hardwood flooring. Complete specifications are given and an attractive wall plank collection is included, plus easy-care instructions to keep your wood floors looking like new. Price is 75¢. Bruce Hardwood Floors.

CARPET SELECTION. For adding color, texture and warmth to a room, Bigelow has designed a group of long-wearing, economically priced carpets for the home. They are presented with facts on color, style and hints on how to put a decorative scheme together in an informative 24-page booklet. Price is 25¢. Bigelow-Sanford.

FLOOR MAINTENANCE. A comprehensive maintenance manual for hardwood flooring — with emphasis on oak — is available. Some points covered are types of finishes and their preservation, and how to remove stains. Price is 25¢. National Oak Flooring Manufacturers' Assn.

TRACK LIGHTING A series of Power-Trac brochures show track-mounted lighting for the home and industry. Provided are a complete description of track lighting systems and a full selection of styled lampholders and accessories. Illumination data and instructions for use of the data are also included. Specifications are provided. Halo Lighting Div. McGraw-Edison.

Carpet is Haddonfield, a Dacron polyester plush with pile yarns spun from a lustrous staple for the effect of washed silk. Rug is by Burlington House Area Rugs. Lees Carpets.

FOLDING REFLECTIONS. Rooms will look larger with closet doors that boast full-length, quality mirrors. Slimfold doors serve a host of decorating needs with other styles that combine louvers, textured panels and mouldings — or plain for simplicity. Evans Door Systems.

EARLY AMERICANA. Lighting fixtures presented in this 64-page catalog are re-creations and adaptations of those used in the 18th and 19th centuries. Fixtures are made of wood and solid brass; antique pewter plating can be special-ordered. Since no work is started until an order is received, fixture sizes can be adapted easily to fit your specifications. Price is $1.50. Authentic Designs.

Evans Door Systems Div. Evans Products Co.

Progress Lighting

Clopay Corp.

DECORATE WITH LIGHTING. A 160-page catalog containing hundreds of fashionable, functional fixtures, from Tiffany styles to a new track lighting system. Includes Early American, Traditional, Contemporary, Oriental and other lighting fashions for every room in your home — and for outdoors. Price is $1. Progress Lighting.

VENTILATED DESIGN. Space Builder shelving creates storage space and hanging space at the same time. The ventilated design allows air to flow through, around and over to fight mildew and stale odors. Shelves are constructed of heavy-duty steel rods with vinyl coating. Closet Maid Corporation.

CONTROL CLUTTER. Ideas are offered in this 16-page fully illustrated booklet entitled "Some Solutions for Clutter." Easy improvement ideas for clearing up closets, putting walls to work as storage units and activating those forgotten nooks and crannies. Price is $1. American Plywood Association.

MODULAR SPACE-SAVERS. Use space wisely with flexible units — single, double, high-boy — that mix and match with a contemporary look. Cabinets, clothes hamper (with removable laundry basket), storage trays and drawers plus an optional make-up tray-mirror for creating a vanity. Snap-on decorative panels add the finishing touch. Literature is 50¢ from Allibert.

DECORATOR LOOK. Prefinished folding doors install in minutes, come in a wide range of styles and shorten easily to fit almost any space. Constructed of heavy gauge vinyl plastic, the doors are woodgrained, textured, woven or color-keyed for today's interiors. Clopay.

CEDAR CLOSETS. Booklet shows you how to build four types of cedar closets — as a bedroom storage wall, and as a free-standing, an entry hall or an under-stairs closet. Lists critical dimensions, giving tips on saving time and money. Price is 25¢. Giles and Kendall.

Please refer to index on page 124 and 125 for manufacturers' addresses.

Planning Aids

FABRIC WALLS. Belgian linen as a versatile wallcovering is the subject of a 16-page color brochure that describes types of linen wallcoverings available plus installation techniques. A second booklet offers instructions on covering walls with linen by stapling. Brochure is 50¢, stapling instructions 25¢. Belgian Linen Association.

Environmental Graphics

MOOD MAKERS. Consider a large-scale graphic to transform your present surroundings to a new environment which encourages personal involvement and expression. More than 40 fresh designs to fit your moods are available — clouds, an aquarium, moon and stars, numbers, Jack and Jill. A packet that displays the colorful patterns is $1.50. Environmental Graphics.

ABOUT PANELING. Whether you're doing it yourself or having it done, "All about Wall Paneling" is a helpful 28-page brochure that takes the mystery out of paneling. Colorfully illustrated with decorating and remodeling suggestions, it features a varied selection of panels, a color guide and helpful installation instructions. Price is 50¢. Champion Building Products.

WALLCOVERING GUIDE. *Living Walls: How to Appreciate and Install Wallpaper and Wall Coverings* is a comprehensive paperback book on wallcoverings by Claire Barrows and William Justin. Fully illustrated with 16 pages of color and over 100 black-and-white photographs, this complete reference book includes a glossary on wallcoverings, definitions and full information on history, manufacturing characteristics and application, plus decorating advice. Price is 50¢. Wallcovering Industry Bureau.

IDEAS GALORE. "Creative Paneling Ideas" features more than 40 beautiful color photos illustrating conventional as well as unusual ways to use paneling in every room of the house. Ideas galore for anyone planning to remodel or redecorate. One section focuses on do-it-yourself ways to produce dramatic results with a minimum of effort. Price is 50¢. Masonite.

Imperial Wallcoverings

Masonite Corp.

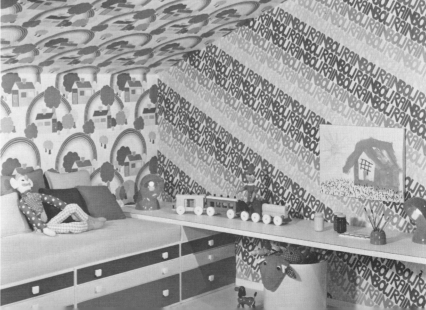

ALL ABOUT MOULDINGS. Plain rooms take on added interest when mouldings are used to create and heighten effects. Some of the mysteries of working with mouldings and planning your own decorative touches are dispelled in "Wood Mouldings," a brochure that discusses their history, uses and modern design. Moulding construction is explained thoroughly and popular patterns (with dimensions) are illustrated. Traditional uses in historic homes are shown and new decorating ideas are given. Price is $1.50. Western Wood Moulding and Millwork Producers.

WINDOW MAGIC. Colorfully illustrated rooms picture Levolor window blinds in a variety of settings in a 24-page booklet. Instructions for measuring, covering (with plastic, fabric, wallpaper or paint), installing, removing and cleaning included. Price is $1. Levolor Lorentzen.

LET YOUR IMAGINATION GO. Today's trend towards freedom and creativity has captured window treatments. *Creative Windows* combines a practical guide to window decorating with pages of colored photos guaranteed to inspire you. The easy-to-follow sequence is organized to lead the reader from basic considerations in color and style through specific rooms to a how-to section for making draperies and selecting the right hardware. Price is $1.55. Kenney.

WOVEN WOODS. A 32-page, full-color book packed with inspiring room settings created by leading designers. Includes complete description and full specifications of woven wood window shades for every application. Price is $1. Graber.

SHADE INSTALLATION. Offering solutions for a varied array of window types and shades, the "Window Shade Primer" shows that there's a shade for every window and a right way to install it. Price is 25¢. Window Shade Mfrs. Assn.

VERTICAL IMAGINATION. Exciting and beautifully photographed is a brochure about louver blinds. Over 30 pages of room scenes show typical uses of the vertical blinds in bedrooms, dens, living, dining and family rooms — plus full-color reproductions of the eight styles and 40 colors available. Accessories and decorator hints included. Price is $1. LouverDrape.

THOUGHT STARTERS. Imaginative, colorful, and brimming with ideas, the "Decorative Coverings Idea Book" opens new ways to be creative in every room with self-adhesive coverings. Fun projects, things to make from scratch and ways to liven what you already have. Decorative coverings come in a wide range of colors and patterns — vinyls, flocks, florals, plaids. These suggestions can be thought-starters for ingenious ideas of your own. Price is $1. Clopay.

Windows without curtains take on special appeal with shades as demonstrated in this cheery child's room. White vinyl Exlite shades insure light control and privacy. Joanna Western Mills.

Please refer to index on pages 124 and 125 for manufacturers' addresses.

Manufacturers' Index

Decorating and Furniture

American Drew
Box 489
North Wilkesboro, NC 28659

Bassett Furniture Industries
Bassett, VA 24055

Bedlam Brass Beds
19-21 Fair Lawn Ave.
Fair Lawn, NJ 07410

Bernhardt Industries
Lenoir, NC 28645

Broyhill Furniture
Box 700
Lenoir, NC 28633

Craft House
Colonial Williamsburg
Foundation
Williamsburg, VA 23185

Davis Cabinet Co.
Box 60444
Nashville, TN 37206

Decorating Data
P.O. Box 60235
Sunnyvale, CA 94088

DeSoto
Box 492
Jackson, MS 39205

Directional Industries
979 Third Ave.
New York, NY 10022

Door Store
3140 M St. NW
Washington, DC 20007

Drexel Furniture Co.
16 Hufman Road
Drexel, NC 28619

Ello Furniture Mfg. Co.
1034 Elm St.
Rockford, IL 61101

Ethan Allen
347 Madison Ave.
New York, NY 10017

Fieldcrest Mills
60 W. 40th St.
New York, NY 10018

Founders Furniture
P.O. Box 339
Thomasville, NC 27360

S. M. Hexter Co.
2810 Superior Ave.
Cleveland, OH 44114

Hickory Manufacturing
Hickory, NC 28601

Instrument Systems Corp.
789 Park Ave.
Huntington, NY 11743

Kemp Furniture Co.
So. Center St.
Goldsboro, NC 27530

Kimball Intl.
1549 Royal St.
Jasper, IN 47546

Kroehler Mfg. Co.
222 E. Fifth Ave.
Naperville, IL 60540

The Lane Co.
Altavista, VA 24517

National Assn. of Furniture Mfrs.
8401 Connecticut Ave., Suite 911
Washington, DC 20015

Nichols & Stone Co.
232 Sherman St.
Gardner, MA 01440

Pennsylvania House Division
General Interiors Corp.
Lewisburg, PA 17837

Pulaski Furniture Corp.
Box 1371
Pulaski, VA 24301

Serta
666 Lake Shore Drive
Chicago, IL 60611

Sico
7525 Cahill Road
Minneapolis, MN 55440

Simmons Co.
One Park Ave.
New York, NY 10016

Spherical Furniture Co.
Box 329
Boone, NC 28607

Stanley Furniture Co.
Stanleytown, VA 24168

Swan Brass Beds
1955 E. 16th St.
Los Angeles, CA 90021

Syroco
Syracuse, NY 13201

Thayer-Coggin, Inc.
P.O. Box 5867
High Point, NC 27261

Thomasville Furniture
Industries
Box 339
Thomasville, NC 27360

Floorcovering

American Enka
530 Fifth Ave.
New York, NY 10036

Armstrong Cork Co.
Lancaster, PA 17604

Bigelow-Sanford
Box 3089
Greenville, SC 29602

Bruce Hardwood Floors
A Triangle Pacific Co.
P.O. Box 171802
Memphis, TN 38117

GAF Corp.
140 West 51 St.
New York, NY 10020

Kodel Div.
Eastman Chemical Products
1133 Ave. of the Americas
New York, NY 10036

Lees Carpets Division
Burlington Industries
Valley Forge Corp. Center
King of Prussia, PA 19406

National Oak Flooring
Mfrs. Assn.
814 Sterick Building
Memphis, TN 38103

Pepperell Carpets
West Point Pepperell
Box 1208
Dalton, GA 39720

Furniture Kits, Plans, and Accessories

American Plywood Assn.
1119 A St.
Tacoma, WA 98401

The Bartley Collection, Ltd.
747 Oakwood Ave.
Lake Forest, IL 60045

Classic Crafts Division
DuBrock Antiques
Box 12
Point Clear, AL 36564

Laura Copenhaver Industries
c/o Rosemont
Box 149
Marion, VA 24354

Country Workshop
95 Rome St.
Newark, NJ 07105

Craftplans
Industrial Blvd.
Rogers, MN 55374

D.O. Unto Others
392 Amsterdam Ave.
New York, NY 10024

Furniture Designs
1425 Sherman Ave.
Evanston, IL 60201

Jenifer House
New Marlboro Stage
Great Barrington, MA 01230

National Assn. of Mirror Mfrs.
5101 Wisconsin Ave.
Washington, DC 20016

Old-House Journal
199 Berkeley Place
Brooklyn, NY 11217

Poster Plus
2906 N. Broadway Ave.
Chicago, IL 60657

Lighting and Electrical Equipment

Authentic Designs
330 East 75th St.
New York, NY 10021

General Electric Co.
Lamp Marketing Dept.
Nela Park
Cleveland, OH 44112

Halo Lighting Division
McGraw-Edison
400 Busse Road
Elk Grove Village, IL 60007

NuTone Division
Scovill
Madison & Red Bank Roads
Cincinnati, OH 45227

Progress Lighting
Erie Avenue and G Street
Philadelphia, PA 19134

Storage and Shelving

Allibert
315 East 62nd St.
New York, NY 10021

Cado
Royal System
57-08 39th Ave.
Woodside, NY 11377

Clopay Corp.
Clopay Square
Cincinnati, OH 45214

Closet Maid Corp.
Box 304/720 SW 17th St.
Ocala, FL 32670

Evans Products Company
Door Systems Division
15500 East Twelve Mile Road
Roseville, MI 48066

Giles & Kendall Co.
Box 188
Huntsville, AL 35804

Schoolfield Furniture Industries
Mullins, SC 29574

Walls and Windows

Belgian Linen Assn.
280 Madison Ave.
New York, NY 10016

California Redwood Association
617 Montgomery St.
San Francisco, CA 94111

Champion Building Products
1 Landmark Square
Stamford, CT 06921

Country Curtains
Stockbridge, MA 01262

Dacor
65 Armory St.
Worcester, MA 01601

Jack Denst Designs
7355 South Exchange Ave.
Chicago, IL 60649

Environmental Graphics
1117 Vicksburg Lane
No. Wayzata, MN 55391

The General Tire & Rubber Co.
1 General St.
Akron, OH 44309

Georgia-Pacific Corp.
900 SW Fifth Ave.
Portland, OR 97204

Graber Co.
Middleton, WI 53562

Imperial Wallcoverings
Collins & Aikman Corp.
3645 Warrensville Center Road
Cleveland, OH 44122

Joanna Western Mills Co.
2141 South Jefferson Street
Chicago, IL 60616

Kenney Mfg. Co.
1000 Jefferson Blvd.
Warwick, RI 02887

Levolor Lorentzen
720 Monroe St.
Hoboken, NJ 07030

LouverDrape
1100 Colorado Ave.
Santa Monica, CA 90401

Masonite Corp.
29 N. Wacker Drive
Chicago, IL 60606

Stauffer Chemical Co.
800 Montrose Ave.
So. Plainfield, NJ 07880

Wallcovering Industry Bureau
1099 Wall Street West
Lyndhurst, NJ 07071

Western Wood Moulding
and Millwork Producers
Box 25278
Portland, OR 97225

Window Shade Mfrs. Assn.
230 Park Ave.
New York, NY 10017

York Wall Paper Co.
York, PA 17405

Photography Credits

American Enka Co.: pages 48 (bottom), 71; American Plywood Assn.: pages 13 (bottom), 79 (bottom); Armstrong Cork Co.: pages 42, 49 (bottom), 63 (top); Bassett Furniture Co.: pages 57 (top), 112; Bernhardt Inds.: page 113; Bigelow-Sanford: page 56 (top); Bruce Hardwood Floors: page 120; Burlington House Carpets: pages 17 (bottom), 43 (top), 52-53, 55 (top); Cado Furniture: pages 50, 73, 74 (bottom), 79 (top), 117; California Redwood Assn.: page 12; Clopay Corp.: page 121; Laura Copenhaver: page 118; Jack Denst Designs: page 98 (bottom); DeSoto: page 115; Directional Inds.: page 104; Drexel Furniture: page 109; Ello Furniture Mfg.: pages 98 (top), 117; Environmental Graphics: page 122; Ethan Allen: page 114; Evans Door Systems: page 121; GAF Corp.: page 54; General Electric Co.: page 18 (bottom); General Tire & Rubber Co.: page 40 (top); Georgia-Pacific Corp.: page 56 (bottom); Halo Lighting: page 120; S. M. Hexter Co.: page 95; Hickory Mfg.: page 106 (bottom); Imperial Wallcovering: page 122; Instrument Systems Corp.: page 80 (bottom); Joanna Western Mills: page 123; Kemp: page 17 (top); Kodel by Eastman Chemical Prods.: pages 34 (bottom), 58 (bottom); Lees Carpets: page 120; Lendon: pages 55, 66 (left); Levolor Lorentzen, Inc.: page 72; Masonite Corp.: page 122; Modern Environments: page 80 (top); Pennsylvania House, General Interiors: page 114; Progress Lighting: page 121; Pulaski Furniture Corp.: page 115; Schoolfield Furniture Inds.: pages 65, 78, 90, 100-101, 117; Sico: page 116; Simmons Co.: pages 10 (right), 14, 36, 47, 57 (bottom), 92, 103 (left), 105 (left), 108 (top); Spherical Furniture Co.: pages 21 (top), 51, 113; Stanley Furniture Co: pages 106 (top), 115; Stauffer Chemical Co.: page 48 (top); Swan (brass beds): page 108 (bottom); Syroco: page 51; Thayer-Coggin, Inc.: page 105 (right); Thomasville Furniture Inds.: page 113; U. S. Plywood Div., Champion International: page 58 (top); West Point Pepperell: page 103 (right); Window Shade Manufacturers Association: pages 10 (left), 33, 37 (bottom), 39, 40 (bottom), 63 (bottom), 66 (right), 74 (top), 75; York Wall Paper Co.: page 34 (top).

PROJECT EDITOR, JOSEPH F. SCHRAM, has been associated with the construction industry for more than 25 years, during which time he has served as a writer and editor of numerous publications. He is the author of several building books and serves as an editorial consultant to manufacturers of building materials, building publications and trade associations.

Contents

About the Authors

Zarina Ibrahim's keen interest in cookery started when she was very young. At the age of twelve, she would watch and help her mother cook. At fourteen, her coconut candy was well known among her fellow students and teachers, and in the area where she lived.

The recipes offered to you in this book have been in the family for many years, handed down by her grandmother, mother and aunts. She learnt the skills and intricacies of North and South Indian cookery from her grandmother and mother, and from an aunt, she learnt the secrets of Indonesian and Malay cookery. Her knowledge of Chinese cookery was gained from a Chinese aunt. She learnt to make Nonya *kueh* through close observation and experiment until she perfected each recipe. A firm believer in the old style of cookery, Zarina is not in favour of using monosodium glutamate or commercial ready-made curry pastes. Given a choice, she would rather use a *batu giling* than a liquidiser.

Zarina's strong religious faith has led her in recent years to take on missionary work in her community and her lectures have made her a well-known speaker and counsellor in both Singaporean and Malaysian Muslim circles. Her creativity in the kitchen has helped feed many pilgrims locally and homesick students in Cairo. Her energy, zest for life, determination and persistence in pursuit of her goals provide her with many examples for her lectures.

Rosalind Mowe is a trained teacher, and taught in St. Theresa's Convent School in Singapore. She read the news over Singapore Broadcasting Corporation's radio broadcasts as a part-timer for a number of years. In August, 1986, she co-authored the Secret Map of Singapore which earned a commendable write-up in the January 11th issue of the New York Times and sold more than fifty thousand copies.

Rosalind's past pupils still recall her teaching days with nostalgia and regularly meet and invite her to their gatherings. She was a popular teacher remembered for her interesting English literature lessons, imparted with firmness and clarity, two traits which have helped to make Zarina's cookbooks so easy to follow. A self taught cook, she progressed from Ellice Handy's Favourite Recipes to Cordon Bleu and realised the need for simple and clear instructions in cookbooks out of sheer necessity.

The creative cooking talents of Zarina and the disciplined and instructional talent of Rosalind were first brought together in 1978 to produce the MPH COOKBOOK. This was followed by, WITH AN EASTERN FLAVOUR, a co-edition produced with Souvenir Press for the United Kingdom and Australian markets and with Barron's Educational for the U.S.A. market. The Malay language edition, RAMPAISARI RASA was published in 1979.

In 1990 they worked together again to produce ZARINA'S HOME COOKING and the Malay language edition, DARI DAPUR ZARINA. Both editions proved to be stunning successes with total sales already at forty thousand copies.

ZARINA'S EASY COOKING and SEMUDAH MASAKAN ZARINA contain almost 170 recipes each of favourite Singapore and Malaysian dishes. In the course of their nearly twenty year collaboration, the most constantly recurring feedback they received about their cookbooks was how easy it was to follow their cooking instructions and recipes. The title EASY COOKING reflects this belief of all followers of Singaporean and Malaysian cooking.

Cooking Tips

CHICKEN

1 If frozen chicken is used, the amount of liquid given in a recipe should be reduced a little.

2 If chicken is fat, reduce the amount of cooking oil or ghee.

3 To cook an authentic Indian chicken curry, the skin of the chicken should be removed and discarded before cooking. Chicken curry will then be less oily and will keep longer.

CHILLIES

1 When buying dried chillies, select the crinkled variety.

2 When a recipe calls for dried chillies to be ground, always soak the chillies in water until they are soft before grinding. If hot water is used, the soaking time will be shorter.

3 For a milder flavour in a curry, remove seeds of fresh or dried chillies.

4 Add or reduce the number of chillies or the amount of chilli powder given in a recipe, according to taste.

5 If a recipe calls for dried chillies to be roasted, do this in a dry pan over low heat stirring now and then to prevent burning.

COCONUT

1 When selecting coconuts, choose older ones which will yield more milk.

2 When extracting coconut milk, add one cup of water to grated coconut at a time and squeeze to extract milk before adding the next cup, even if recipe calls for 4 cups of water.

FRESH TURMERIC (*kunyit*)

The older root, which is dark in colour, is preferable.

LEMON GRASS (*serai*)

Only about 6-7cm (2 $\frac{1}{2}$ - 3in) of the root end should be used.

LENGKUAS (*botanical: galangal*)

If lengkuas needs to be ground, buy a tender piece that is pinkish in colour.

LENTIL (*dhal*)

Always select the larger variety; soak for about 2 hours in cold water before using, then wash and remove loose skin.

TAMARIND

1 Select the darker variety.

2 To make tamarind juice, combine specified amount of water and tamarind pulp, mix with fingers and strain.

GENERAL

1 If while cooking curry is drying up fast and you wish to add more water, make sure *warm* water is used.

2 Indians use yoghurt to tenderise meat; add about 1 tbsp to 450g of meat and marinate for about 20-30 minutes before cooking.

3 One of the secrets of a good curry lies in the quality and amount of spices used. It is preferable, therefore, that you prepare your own ground spices or buy them from a reliable source. Very often, commercial curry powders are adulterated with rice or maize flour and do not contain the pure ingredients.

4 Care of the griddle (*tawa*) used for cooking Chapati, Dosai, Roti and Roti Jala:-

i) Wash new griddle with warm water.

ii) Season the new griddle by using about a handful of grated coconut. Fry this on griddle over low heat, making use of every part of the griddle. Keep stirring coconut for about 40 minutes then discard coconut. Next, heat a tablespoon of cooking oil on griddle, break an egg and spread it all over. Discard egg when it is cooked and wipe surface of griddle. It is now ready for use. After this, the griddle should *never* be washed. After use, merely wipe over with a dry cloth or a paper towel. If at any time food sticks to it during use, repeat egg treatment.

Note on Malay Spelling: the revised form of spelling introduced in 1973 has been used in this book. Thus, *blachan* is now spelled *blacan*, *kachang* as *kacang*, etc., but of course the pronunciation of these words remains the same.

5

Weights & Measures

			metric equivalent	round metric equivalent
1 metric teaspoon holds 5ml	1 kati	(16 tah)	605g	600g
1 metric tablespoon holds 15ml	3/4 kati	(12 tah)	454g	450g
1 metric cup holds 250ml	1/2 kati	(8 tah)	302g	300g
4 metric cups = 1 litre	1/4 kati	(4 tah)	151g	150g
		(2 tah)	76g	80g
		(1 tah)	38g	40g

Abbreviations

		imperial		
kilogram	kg			
gram	g			
centimetre	cm	1 lb	(16 oz)	453.6g	450g
teaspoon	tsp	3/4 lb	(12 oz)	340.2g	340g
tablespoon	tbsp	1/2 lb	(8 oz)	226.8g	230g
millilitre	ml	1/4 lb	(4 oz)	113.4g	120g
litre	l		(2 oz)	56.7g	60g
			(1 oz)	28.3g	30g

Curry Powders

SPICES FOR NORTH INDIAN COOKING

1. **Dried Chilli** - wipe clean, break or cut into pcs and roast in dry pan till fragrant. Grind coarsely

2. **Ketumbar seeds (Coriander)** - remove stalks and grit, roast in dry pan till fragrant. Grind coarsely.

3. **Jintan Puteh Seeds (cumin)** - remove stalks and grit, roast in dry pan till fragrant. Grind coarsely.

Store each separately in air tight container in cool dry place and use as necessary. Will keep for 2-3 weeks.

GARAM MASALA
(North Indian)

Ingredients:
- 3 tbsp ketumbar seeds (coriander)
- 1 tsp jintan puteh seeds (cumin)
- 1/2 tsp sajira seeds (dark fine cumin)
- 1/2 tsp black peppercorns
- 1 stick cinnamon (4cm) - break into pcs
- 4 cardamoms
- 4 cloves

Method:
Clean seeds, (remove stalks, stones and grit). Roast seeds and peppercorns in dry pan till medium brown and fragrant. Roast cinnamon, cardamom and cloves. Cool thoroughly then grind till almost fine.

Garam Masala is usually used in small amounts in cooking or for sprinkling over cooked food.

MEAT CURRY POWDER
(South Indian)

Ingredients:
5 tbsp ketumbar seeds (coriander)
1 tsp jintan manis seeds (fennel)
$\frac{1}{2}$ tsp jintan puteh seeds (cumin)
$\frac{1}{2}$ tsp black peppercorns
1 stick cinnamon (2 cm length)
2 cardamoms
2 cloves
16 dried chillies - wipe and cut or break into pcs.
Roast separately till med. brown.

Method:
Remove stalks, stones and grit from seeds. Roast all the above (except chilli) in dry pan till medium brown and fragrant. Cool then mix roasted chilli with other spices and grind fine. Add $\frac{1}{2}$ tsp turmeric powder to ground mixture. Mix well and store in air tight containers.

FISH CURRY POWDER
(South Indian)

Ingredients:
5 tbsp ketumbar seeds (coriander)
1 tsp jintan manis seeds (fennel)
$\frac{1}{2}$ tsp jintan puteh seeds (cumin)
$\frac{1}{2}$ tsp black peppercorns
16 dried chillies - wipe and cut or break into pcs.
Roast separately till medium brown.

Method:
Remove stalks, stones and grit from seeds. Roast seeds and peppercorns in dry pan till medium brown and fragrant. Cool then mix with roasted chilli and grind fine. Add $\frac{1}{2}$ tsp turmeric (kunyit) powder to ground mixture. Mix well and store in air tight container.

SRI LANKAN CURRY POWDER

Ingredients:
2 tbsp ketumbar seeds (coriander)
1 tsp jintan puteh seeds (cumin)
$\frac{1}{2}$ tsp jintan manis seeds (fennel)
$\frac{1}{4}$ tsp alba
$\frac{1}{2}$ tsp black peppercorns
1 stick cinnamon (3 cm)
10 dried chillies - wipe clean, break or cut into pcs.
Roast separately till fragrant

Method:
Remove stalks, stones and grit from seeds. Roast all the above ingredients (except chilli) in dry pan till dark brown and fragrant.
Cool then mix roasted chilli with other spices and grind fine. Add $\frac{1}{2}$ tsp turmeric (kunyit) powder to ground mixture. Mix well and store in air tight container.

KORMA CURRY POWDER

Ingredients:
3 tbsp ketumbar seeds (coriander)
1 tsp jintan puteh seeds (cumin)
1 tsp white peppercorns
2 sticks cinnamon (each 2 cm length)
2 cardamoms
2 cloves

Method:
Remove stalks, stone and grit from seeds. Roast all the above in dry pan till medium brown and fragrant. Cool then grind fine. Add $\frac{1}{4}$ tsp turmeric (kunyit) powder to ground mixture, mix well and store in air tight container.

Preparing Curry Powders
If making large quantity, send spice seeds to the mill for grinding. For small quantity, use spice mill or coffee grinder. Cool spice powder well after grinding before storing in air tight containers. Once a week, open containers to air curry powder.

The length of time curry powder lasts depends very much on the quality of spices used.

Grind both the seeds and outer layer of cardamoms.

Step by Step

PULOT KUKUS

Ingredients: For the filling:
- ☐ *³/₄ cup brown sugar*
- ☐ *¹/₂ cup water*
- ☐ *1 cup grated coconut*

For the dough:
- ☐ *2 cups glutinous rice flour (tepong pulot)*
- ☐ *230g grated coconut - add ¹/₂ cup water and, using a fine tea towel, squeeze coconut to extract ¹/₂ cup thick coconut milk*
- ☐ *¹/₂ tsp salt*
- ☐ *¹/₂ tsp green food colouring*
- ☐ *banana leaf cut into 20 rectangular pieces (4 x 5 cm or 1¹/₂ x 2 in)*

1 Filling:
Put sugar and water in a saucepan. Heat till sugar dissolves. Strain syrup and put back in saucepan. Add grated coconut. Cook over low heat, stirring all the time, till mixture is thick and moist. Cool.

2 Dough:
Put glutinous rice flour in a bowl. Add salt. Add colouring to coconut milk and pour into flour. Mix into a soft dough.

3
Put a small lump of dough on a piece of banana leaf, flatten it a little, add a spoonful of coconut filling. Wrap dough around filling to form an oval shape about 4 to 5cm (1¹/₂ to 2in) long.

4
Make leaf design with a tart pincher or trace design with a skewer. Steam for about ¹/₂ hour. Serve while still warm. Makes about 20.

STEAMED NASI LEMAK WITH IKAN BILIS SAMBAL
(the original recipe)

Ingredients for rice:

- ☐ 500g rice - wash and drain
- ☐ 300g grated coconut (without skin) ⎫ mix to obtain equal
- ☐ 625-650ml water ⎬ amount of milk
- ☐ salt to taste
- ☐ 1 pc ginger (size of walnut) - bruise
- ☐ 3 fragrant screwpine leaves (daun pandan) - wash and tie into knot

Method:

Combine all the above ingredients in a pot. Bring to the boil then simmer till rice is cooked.

- ☐ 1 cucumber - peel then slice thick
- ☐ Banana leaves - 6 to 8 rectangular pieces (35cm x 25cm)
  16 square pieces (8cm x 8cm)
  Scald leaves with hot water then dry them

Ingredients for Sambal:

Grind fine

- ☐ 30 dried chillies - soak till soft
- ☐ 2 onions
- ☐ 1 clove garlic
- ☐ 2 level tbsp dried silver fish (fine ikan bilis) - soak for 10 to 15 mins

If using liquidiser, use sufficient water to make a thick paste.

- ☐ 5 tbsp oil
- ☐ $^{1}/_{2}$ level tbsp tamarind pulp ⎫ mix and strain
- ☐ 4 tbsp water ⎬ to obtain juice
- ☐ 2 tbsp sugar
- ☐ salt to taste
- ☐ 50g dried anchovies (dried ikan bilis) - remove head, split in two, wash, drain and dry well
- ☐ 2 tbsp coconut crumbs - see recipe for COCONUT CRUMBS (can be cooked a day beforehand)

Method:

Heat oil sufficient to fry ikan bilis till lightly brown but not crisp. Drain and keep aside.

Heat 5 tbsp oil, add ground ingredients and cook till fragrant. Add tamarind juice, sugar and salt. Stir well then add fried ikan bilis and coconut crumbs. Cook for a further 5 mins. till sambal is of a thick consistency.

To serve:

Wrap rice and sambal in banana leaf (see Step By Step guide)

Alternatively, put a piece of banana leaf on a large platter, dish rice on leaf, arrange cucumber slices along the edge around rice and serve sambal in a separate dish.

Note: Nasi Lemak cooked this way is traditionally served for breakfast

How to Wrap Nasi Lemak

1
Put one serving of rice on a banana leaf

2
Lift the two lengths of banana leaf over rice and press so that the mound of rice becomes compact

3
Put a square of banana leaf over rice and a large teaspoonful of Ikan Bilis Sambal on leaf

4
Put a square of banana leaf over Sambal, press down a little and put 2 slices of cucumber on leaf

5
Fold the two lengths at one end so they overlap

6
Hold up packet and tuck end under

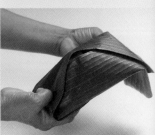

7
Fold other end and tuck as in 5 and 6

ROTI JALA

Ingredients:

- [ ] *450g grated coconut (without skin) - add 3 cups water and extract 4 cups milk*
- [ ] *450g plain flour - sieve*
- [ ] *1 tsp salt*
- [ ] *2 eggs*
- [ ] *a drop of yellow food colouring (optional)*
- [ ] *ghee or cooking oil to grease pan*

TO FRY: use medium size frying pan or hot plate. A non-stick frying pan is ideal.

COOKING TIP: Substitute coconut milk with:-
a) 1 large tin of evaporated milk mixed with $2\frac{1}{2}$ cups water
   or
b) 4 cups skimmed milk

To make a brush: take 2 pandan leaves, fold them in two, secure one end with a rubber band and cut the other end to make the brush. Use this to brush pan with oil.

1
Put flour and salt in a bowl. Make a well in the center. Break eggs into well. Add colouring to coconut milk and pour half the milk into the flour. Stir, drawing in flour from the sides. When mixture is smooth, add the rest of the coconut milk. Stir well.

2
Strain batter using a ladle to push batter through strainer. The batter must be neither too thick nor too thin.

3
Heat pan. Brush pan with ghee or cooking oil. Dip Jala cup into batter and quickly pour batter into pan in circles till a lacy pancake is formed. While pancake is cooking, dab a little oil over it. Remove from heat as soon as firm.

4
To fold: Bring 2 sides of the pancake to meet at the center. Do the same with the other 2 sides.

5
Fold once more to form a small roll. Arrange pancakes on a plate. Serve with Chicken Coconut Milk Curry.

MURUKKU

Ingredients:

- ☐ *600g gram flour (besan)*
- ☐ *1 tbsp omum seeds - sieve and remove stones*
- ☐ *1 slightly heaped tbsp chilli powder*
- ☐ *2 slightly heaped tsp turmeric powder*
- ☐ *1 tsp salt, mix with 300 ml water*
- ☐ *oil for deep frying*

Note: Store the cooled murukku in an air tight container.

1
Dough press with various discs.
Select disc with bigger holes for
Murukku.
The disc with the smaller holes is
used for making Putu Mayam

2
In a large bowl, put gram flour,
omum seeds, chilli and turmeric
powder. Mix well.

3
Add water to which salt has been
added. Mix till dough is smooth. Put
a handful of dough into dough press.

4
Heat oil in a wok. Lower murukku
strands into hot oil by turning
handle of dough press and simultaneously moving the dough press in a
circular motion over wok to make a
coil of murukku.
Break off strands of dough with a
sweep of your hand when a large
enough coil is formed in the oil.
Fry till crisp and drain.
Repeat till all the dough is used.

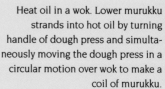

PUTU BAMBOO

Ingredients:
- [ ] *230g rice flour*
- [ ] *1 tsp salt*
- [ ] *3 tbsp water*
- [ ] *1 $\frac{1}{2}$ cups grated coconut (remove skin) - set aside $\frac{1}{2}$ cup*

NOTE: Aluminium Putu Bamboo steamers are available in Indian General Stores. The steamer is made up of three parts, the pot for water, the funnel with a disc inside and a lid. Wrap a strip of cotton or towel (a strip from an old tea towel will do) around the base of the funnel so that it fits snugly into the pot and seals the container. Originally, thick bamboos were used as they were easily available. The bamboos were fitted snugly into a mug or kettle of water. Hence the name Putu Bamboo.

1

Dissolve salt in water and sprinkle over rice flour. Mix to get a crumbly texture. Add 1 cup coconut and mix well.

2

Put 1 tbsp coconut (from $\frac{1}{2}$ cup set aside) into funnel

3

Add 3 heaped tbsp of rice flour-coconut mixture

4

Repeat steps 2 and 3 till rice flour-coconut mixture is used up. Make sure the last layer is of coconut. Fill pot with water and boil. Fit funnel into pot of boiling water and cook till steam appears.

5

When cooked, remove putu from funnel by pushing the disc at the base using the thick round handle of a wooden spoon or any similar object. Serve with bananas and brown sugar.

HOW TO CLEAN A SQUID (SOTONG)

1
Whole squid before cleaning

2
Take squid in one hand, hold
head firmly with the other hand
and gently ease it out of the body

3
Push down tentacles and cut off
hard knob visible on the top

4
Cut out eyes

5
Cut off soft jelly-like pieces at the
opposite end of tentacles

6
Gently remove ink bag taking care
not to pierce it

7
Hold body in one hand and pull
out soft bone from body with the
other
8
Peel off mottled skin from body

Fried Bee Hoon - Indian style

Chicken Bee Hoon - Briani style

20

BAKED MACARONI

Ingredients:

- [ ] *300g minced beef*
- [ ] *$1/2$ tsp pepper*
- [ ] *1 tsp chilli powder*
- [ ] *$1/2$ tsp turmeric powder*
- [ ] *2 tsp coriander (ketumbar) powder*
- [ ] *salt to taste*
- [ ] *2 red chillies - thinly sliced, slantwise*
- [ ] *1 slice ginger (2cm or $3/4$ in thick)* ⎫
- [ ] *1 clove garlic* ⎬ *grind to a fine paste*
- [ ] *2 tbsp cooking oil*
- [ ] *230g pipe macaroni*
- [ ] *2 spring onions* ⎫
- [ ] *3 sprigs small coriander leaves* ⎬ *chop fine*
- [ ] *3 sprigs big coriander leaves* ⎭
- [ ] *$1/2$ tbsp margarine*
- [ ] *3 eggs - beaten with a little salt*

Method:

Mix minced beef with ginger-garlic paste, pepper, chilli, turmeric, coriander powder and salt.

Heat oil, add beef, fry until liquid is absorbed, then remove from heat.

Bring a pan of water to the boil. When actively boiling, add macaroni and cook for about 12 minutes.

Spread the margarine in an ovenproof dish, then put about two-thirds of the macaroni to form the first layer.

Spread meat, chopped spring onions and coriander leaves over macaroni to form a second layer; spoon one beaten egg over this. Finally, cover this layer with the rest of the macaroni and spoon two beaten eggs over this. Dot the top layer with margarine and bake in moderate oven for about 20 minutes.

Serve with cucumber salad.

Baked Macaroni

FRIED BEE HOON - INDIAN STYLE
(Rice Noodles)

Ingredients:

- [ ] *1 onion* ⎫
- [ ] *1 clove garlic* ⎬ *grind to a fine paste*
- [ ] *16 dried chillies - break each into 3 - 4 pieces and soak* ⎭
- [ ] *4 tbsp oil*
- [ ] *2 hard beancurd (taukwa) - cut into small squares*
- [ ] *salt to taste*
- [ ] *2 tbsp tomato sauce*
- [ ] *$1/2$ tbsp dark soya sauce*
- [ ] *4 medium sized tomatoes - slice thickly*
- [ ] *2 red chillies* ⎫
- [ ] *2 green chillies* ⎬ *slice*
- [ ] *2-3 eggs - beat lightly*
- [ ] *300g spring greens (chye sim) - cut into 3cm ($1 1/4$ in) lengths*
- [ ] *300g bean sprouts - remove tails*
- [ ] *3 medium sized potatoes - boil and cut into slices 0.5 cm ($1/4$ in) lenghts*
- [ ] *230g rice vermicelli (bee hoon) - soak for 15-20 mins then cut into shorter strands*

Method:

Heat oil, add ground ingredients and fry till fragrant. Add taukwa, salt, tomato sauce and dark soya sauce and stir. Add tomatoes and sliced chillies, stir, then push ingredients to the side of the pan.

Pour the eggs into the middle and let eggs cook. Mix with other ingredients in the pan, then add chye sim, bean sprouts and boiled potatoes, stirring after each addition. Finally, add bee hoon, stir, mixing it with all the other ingredients.

Serve with sliced cucumber, tomato sauce and cut lime.

CHICKEN BEE HOON BRIANI STYLE

Ingredients:

- [ ] 450g rice vermicelli (bee hoon) - soak in water till soft
- [ ] 2 tsp yellow food colouring - sprinkle over bee hoon and mix evenly
- [ ] 2 tsp white peppercorns - grind fine
- [ ] 1 chicken weighing about 1.5kg - cut into pieces and season with ground pepper; leave for 10-15 mins and deep fry till golden brown
- [ ] 3 tbsp ghee or cooking oil

Grind to a smooth paste:

- [ ] 2 slices ginger - each 1cm ($1/2$ in) thick
- [ ] 3 cloves garlic
- [ ] 6 dried chillies - soak

- [ ] salt to taste
- [ ] 4 tomatoes - half and slice thinly
- [ ] 1 red chilli ⎫
- [ ] 1 green chilli ⎬ slit into two
- [ ] 1 tbsp meat curry powder
- [ ] 1 bunch big coriander leaves
- [ ] 230 ml (1 scant cup) water

For garnishing:

- [ ] 10 shallots - slice thinly and deep fry till golden brown
- [ ] mint leaves
- [ ] small can of green peas - drain

Method:

Heat ghee or oil in a frying pan and fry ground ingredients until fragrant. Add salt, tomatoes, chillies, curry powder and coriander leaves. Fry for 2-3 minutes then add water.

When boiling, add fried chicken and mix thoroughly, making sure chicken is well coated with fried ingredients. Remove chicken, leaving the spices in the pan. Add coloured bee hoon to pan, stir fry and mix well, adding salt if necessary. Put chicken back in pan and mix.

Serve on a bed of lettuce and garnish with green peas, fried shallots and mint leaves.

Serve with pineapple and cucumber salad if desired.

Fried Vegetarian Rice

Omelette with Minced Meat Filling

FRIED VEGETARIAN RICE

Ingredients:

- [ ] 2 tbsp sesame oil
- [ ] 2 tbsp cooking oil

Slice finely:

- [ ] 2 red chillies
- [ ] 2 green chillies
- [ ] 1 medium onion - half then slice
- [ ] 2 cloves garlic

- [ ] 1g black fungus - soak, clean, remove hard stump and drain
- [ ] $1/4$ cup water
- [ ] pepper
- [ ] salt to taste
- [ ] 1 tbsp light soya sauce
- [ ] 100g carrot - cut into strips
- [ ] 100g french beans - top and tail then slice fine diagonally
- [ ] 300g cooked rice

For garnishing:

- [ ] 2 stalks spring onion ⎫
- [ ] 2 stalks coriander leaves ⎬ chop

Method:

Heat sesame and cooking oil. Add sliced ingredients and fry till fragrant. Add black fungus, stir then add water, salt, pepper and soya sauce. Stir then add carrot and beans. When vegetables are almost cooked, add cooked rice. Mix well.

Garnish with spring onions and coriander leaves.

Omelette With Minced Meat Filling

Ingredients:

- [ ] 5 eggs - *beat well and season with salt and pepper*
- [ ] 1 big onion - *chop*
- [ ] 100g minced beef
- [ ] 1 tbsp tomato puree
- [ ] 4 sprigs mint - *chop fine*
- [ ] 1 tsp black peppercorns - *grind fine and add to minced beef*
- [ ] salt to taste
- [ ] 50g chives - *chop fine*
- [ ] 1 small green pepper (capsicum) - *cut into thin strips* ⎫
- [ ] 100g carrot - *shred* ⎬ mix
- [ ] 2 tomatoes - *cut in half, remove seeds then slice fine* ⎭
- [ ] 1 tbsp oil

Method:

Fry onions in 2 -3 tbsp oil till soft and brown. Drain and keep aside.

In separate pan or wok, put minced beef. Stir over heat, without using any oil, till meat is dry and crumbly. Add salt then tomato puree; stir, add fried onions and mint and mix well.

In large deep omelette pan, heat oil.

Pour 2 ladles egg into pan; over this, sprinkle 2 tbsp cooked minced beef, 2 tbsp chives and 2 tbsp carrot-capsicum mixture. Pour sufficient egg over this to cover the vegetables. Repeat with a layer of meat and vegetable followed by a layer of egg. Arrange tomato slices over last layer and cook over slow fire. If the top is still wet when the rest of the omelette is cooked, put it under the grill for a few minutes. Cut into wedges and serve.

Fried Beef Kwei Teow (Malay Style)

Ingredients:

- [ ] 1kg kwei teow (flat rice noodles)
- [ ] 300g shredded beef (tenderloin or fillet)
- [ ] 200g bean sprouts - *remove tails*
- [ ] 300g shrimps - *remove shell and devein*
- [ ] 200g kangkong (water convolvulus)
  - break or cut into 5cm lengths
- [ ] 2 tbsp dark soya sauce
- [ ] 6 tbsp oil

Grind finely:

- [ ] 10 dried chillies - *soak to soften*
- [ ] 5 red chillies ⎫
- [ ] 1 onion ⎬ *cut into pieces*
- [ ] 2 cloves garlic ⎭

Method:

Heat oil, add ground ingredients and fry till fragrant. Add beef, mix well with chilli mixture then add soya sauce. Stir well. Add shrimps, cook for a few minutes then add kwei teow. Mix well. Add kangkong and bean sprouts. Keep stirring till vegetables are cooked.

Chicken Macaroni In Tomato Broth

Ingredients:

- [ ] 1 kg chicken breast - *cut into bite size pieces*
- [ ] 4 medium tomatoes - *remove seeds, cut into pieces then liquidise*
- [ ] 2 cloves garlic - *add to tomato and liquidise*
- [ ] $^1/_2$ tbsp ground black pepper
- [ ] 1 tbsp butter
- [ ] 6 tbsp tomato puree
- [ ] 800 ml water
- [ ] 1 medium carrot - *peel then cut into small cubes*
- [ ] 50g green peas
- [ ] Juice of 1 lemon
- [ ] salt to taste

Method:

Combine chicken with ground tomato and pepper. Heat butter, add chicken-tomato mixture and stir well. Add tomato puree, water, carrot and green peas. Bring to the boil, add lemon juice and salt and stir well. Continue to simmer till chicken and carrots are soft.

Note: This is a bland dish suitable for children.

BEE HOON SALADO

Ingredients:
- ☐ *400g bee hoon (rice vermicelli) - soak in cold water for 15-20 mins. then scald and drain. Cut into shorter lengths.*
- ☐ *12 tbsp oil*
- ☐ *2 hard bean curd (taukwa) - cut into small cubes, deep fry, drain and keep aside*

Ingredients for frying:
- ☐ *2 green chillies* ⎫
- ☐ *2 red chillies* ⎬ *chop fine*
- ☐ *4 cloves garlic* ⎪
- ☐ *1 big onion* ⎭

- ☐ *salt to taste*
- ☐ *50g dried lily buds (kim chiam) - tie each into a knot*
- ☐ *50g Chinese mushroom* ⎫
- ☐ *50g black fungus* ⎬ *Soak till soft and cut into strips*
- ☐ *50g dried bean curd skin* ⎭
- ☐ *400 ml water*
- ☐ *100g french beans - slice diagonally*
- ☐ *150g carrot - cut into fine strips*
- ☐ *150g cauliflower - cut into florets*
- ☐ *4 tbsp light soya sauce*
- ☐ *200g spring greens (chye sim) - break or cut into 4cm lengths; separate leaves from stalks.*
- ☐ *pepper*

Method:

Heat oil, add ingredients for frying and salt. Fry till fragrant. Add dried lily buds, mushroom, black fungus and bean curd skin. Mix well. Add water. When boiling, add beans, carrot, cauliflower, soya sauce and pepper. Stir well and cook for a while. Add bee hoon. Mix well. Add stalks of spring greens first, cook for a while then add leaves. Stir well. Add fried taukwa cubes and mix. Serve with pickled green chillies.

Mee Serani

Fried Beef Kwei Teow - Malay style

Chicken Macaroni in Tomato broth

Pickled Chilli

Pineapple Sambal

Bee Hoon Salado

MEE SERANI

Ingredients:

- [ ] 500g fresh yellow round noodles - cut into shorter lengths and rinse quickly under running water
- [ ] 200g sotong (squid) - clean and cut into rings
- [ ] 200g shrimps - remove head and shell and devein
- [ ] $\frac{1}{2}$ cup water
- [ ] salt to taste
- [ ] 200g spring greens(chye sim) - break into 4cm lengths separate leaves from stalks
- [ ] 100g bean sprouts (taugeh) - remove tails
- [ ] 5 tbsp oil
- [ ] 6 red chillies ⎫
- [ ] 1 onion ⎬ grind finely
- [ ] 2 cloves garlic ⎪
- [ ] 1 tsp blacan ⎭

Method:

Heat oil, add ground ingredients and fry till fragrant. Add water, stir into mixture. Add sotong, shrimps and salt and cook for 5 mins. Add noodles, stir then add spring greens and bean sprouts. Mix well.

Ingredients for Pineapple Sambal:

- [ ] 4 red chillies
- [ ] 1 clove garlic
- [ ] 1 pc blacan (2 x 2 x 1 cm) - dry roast
- [ ] 1 tbsp sugar
- [ ] $\frac{1}{4}$ small pineapple - chop very fine
- [ ] salt to taste

Method:

Grind chilli, garlic and roasted blacan till fine. Stir in sugar and salt. Add pineapple and mix. Serve with noodles.

KAI LAN WITH SLICED FISH

Ingredients:

- [ ] 300g kai lan (Chinese Kale) - separate leaves from stalks and cut or break into 5cm lengths
- [ ] 100g ikan kurau (threadfin or red snapper) - slice and marinate with 1 tbsp light soya sauce and pepper
- [ ] 1 red chilli ⎫
- [ ] 3-4 shallots ⎬ slice
- [ ] 2 cloves garlic ⎪
- [ ] 3 tbsp oil ⎭

Method:

Heat oil, add sliced ingredients. When fragrant, add fish and stir. Add vegetable stalks, sprinkle some water over, stir and cook for a minute or two. Add leaves, stir and mix well. Vegetable must not be overcooked.

Spinach with Shredded Beef

*Chye Sim with Straw Mushrooms
and Carrots*

Kai Lan with Sliced Fish

27

SPINACH WITH SHREDDED BEEF

Ingredients:
- ☐ 3 shallots
- ☐ 1 red chilli } slice
- ☐ 1 garlic
- ☐ 1cm ginger - shred or cut into strips
- ☐ 200g beef (fillet) - slice thin
- ☐ 300g spinach - separate stalks from leaves and cut or break into 5cm lengths
- ☐ 2 tbsp light soya sauce
- ☐ 1/4 cup water
- ☐ salt to taste
- ☐ 3 tbsp oil

Method:
Heat oil. Add shallots, chilli, garlic and ginger. Fry till fragrant then add beef. Stir well. Add soya sauce, water and salt. Add vegetable stalks, cook a little then add leaves. Do not overcook vegetables.

CHYE SIM WITH STRAW MUSHROOMS AND CARROTS

Ingredients:
- ☐ 2 cloves garlic } slice
- ☐ 3 shallots
- ☐ 1cm piece ginger - shred or cut into strips
- ☐ 200g spring greens (chye sim) - separate stalks from leaves and cut or break into 5cm lengths
- ☐ 100g carrot - peel and slice at an angle (not too thick)
- ☐ 1/2 cup straw mushroom - use whole
- ☐ 1 tbsp light soya sauce
- ☐ pepper
- ☐ 1 tsp cornflour - mix with 2 tbsp water
- ☐ 2 tbsp oil
- ☐ 1 tbsp sesame oil

Method:
Heat sesame and cooking oil, add garlic, shallots and ginger. When fragrant, add carrot and mushroom. Cook for a few minutes. Add soya sauce and pepper. Add vegetable stalks, then leaves, sprinkle a little water over and cook rapidly. Add cornflour mixture and stir.

INDIAN MUTTON SOUP

Ingredients:
- ☐ 450g mutton - cut into small squares
- ☐ 2 tsp white pepper
- ☐ 4 tbsp coriander (ketumbar) powder
- ☐ 1 fresh green chilli - slash
- ☐ salt to taste

Grind to a smooth paste:
- ☐ 2 slices ginger - each 1cm (1/2 in) thick
- ☐ 3-4 cloves garlic
- ☐ 2 tsp white poppy seeds (kas kas)
- ☐ 1 tsp cumin (jintan puteh)
- ☐ 4-5 tbsp oil

Ingredients for frying:
- ☐ 1 stick cinnamon
- ☐ 3-4 cloves
- ☐ 2-3 cardamoms
- ☐ 1 medium sized onion - slice thinly
- ☐ 7-8 cups water

For garnishing:
- ☐ 4-5 spring onions - chop coarsely
- ☐ 8-10 shallots - peel, slice thinly and fry till golden brown; set aside

Method:
Combine mutton with ground ingredients, pepper, coriander, green chilli and salt in a bowl and mix evenly.

Heat oil, then add ingredients for frying. Fry till golden brown, add meat and fry till fragrant then leave to cook for 5-8 minutes. Add water and boil till meat is tender.

Garnish with fried shallots and chopped spring onion.

Serve with French loaf or toast.

PEANUT SAUCE DRESSING

Ingredients:

- [ ] *¹/₂ cup peanuts - dry fry till brown, remove skin and grind coarsely*
- [ ] *1 potato (or sweet potato) about 50-70g in weight - peel, boil and mash*
- [ ] *3 tbsp boiled water - add to mashed potato and mix well*
- [ ] *12 dried chillies - cut and soak in hot water to soften* } *grind fine*
- [ ] *2 cloves garlic*
- [ ] *3 tbsp brown sugar*
- [ ] *¹/₂ cup water*
- [ ] *salt to taste*
- [ ] *1 tbsp tomato puree*
- [ ] *1 tbsp vinegar*

Method:

In a saucepan, put chilli-garlic paste, brown sugar, water and salt and tomato puree. Bring to the boil, stirring to dissolve sugar. Add vinegar and mashed potato (push potato through a sieve). Reduce heat and boil stirring all the time till a little thick. Add ground peanuts, stir and remove from heat.

Note: If using sweet potato, reduce the amount of sugar.

SAUCE FOR BEEF ROLL

Ingredients:

- [ ] *4 tbsp tomato sauce*
- [ ] *2 cups water*
- [ ] *¹/₂ tsp pepper*
- [ ] *salt to taste*
- [ ] *1 tsp golden bread crumbs*
- [ ] *120g green peas*
- [ ] *4-5 medium sized tomatoes - quartered*

Method:

Add ¹/₂ cup water to pan juices. Stir to mix, then pour into a saucepan and add tomato sauce, rest of water, bread crumbs, pepper and salt. Bring to the boil, then add green peas and tomato quarters. Bring back to the boil and remove from heat. Pour sauce over rolls just before serving.

STUFFED BEEF ROLL

Ingredients:

- [ ] *2 large carrots - peel and grate coarsely*
- [ ] *4 large potatoes - boil and peel (add a pinch of salt to water for boiling)*
- [ ] *¹/₄ tsp salt*
- [ ] *¹/₂ tsp pepper*
- [ ] *8 large thin slices of topside beef*
- [ ] *4 tsp butter or margarine*

Method:

Mash potatoes, add pepper and salt.

Lay a piece of beef flat on a board, spread a thin layer of mashed potatoes over it. Put 1 tbsp grated carrot over the potato and fold to form a roll. Secure with thread. Repeat till all the pieces of beef are used. Spread 2 teaspoons of butter or margarine on a baking tray. Place rolls in tray and dot each roll with a little butter or margarine. Put the tray under the grill. After about 10 minutes turn rolls over, grill for another 5-8 minutes till meat is brown.

Remove beef rolls from tray. Reserve juices in tray for sauce.

Note: Beef rolls may be cooked for about 20 minutes in a moderately hot oven (200°C or 400°F).

BAMIAH
(Arab Dish)

Ingredients:

- [ ] *600g topside beef - cut into large cubes*

Roast in dry pan over low heat:

- [ ] *3 tbsp coriander (ketumbar)*
- [ ] *2 tsp cumin (jintan puteh) seeds*
- [ ] *1 tsp fennel (jintan manis) seeds*
- [ ] *12 dried chillies*

- [ ] *1 tsp white peppercorns*
- [ ] *1 piece dried turmeric (size of almond)*
- [ ] *4-5 cloves garlic*
- [ ] *1 piece ginger (size of walnut)* } *grind to a fine paste*
- [ ] *salt to taste*
- [ ] *3 tbsp ghee or 5 tbsp oil*
- [ ] *2 cups water*
- [ ] *1 tbsp tomato paste*
- [ ] *1 medium sized onion - slice thinly*
- [ ] *1 stick cinnamon 5cm (2in) length* } *ingredients to*
- [ ] *3 cardamoms* *be fried*
- [ ] *3 cloves*
- [ ] *4 tbsp ghee*
- [ ] *300g small ladies fingers (okra) - cut off top and tail and slash half way from tail end up*
- [ ] *300g small tomatoes - cut off top*
- [ ] *green peas for garnishing*

Method:

Grind coriander, cumin, fennel, dried chillies and turmeric finely, adding peppercorns last.

Combine meat in a bowl with ground ingredients, ginger-garlic paste and salt.

Heat ghee or oil, add ingredients to be fried. When onions are a little brown, add meat and fry until fragrant, then add water combined with tomato paste. Cover and simmer till meat is tender, stirring occasionally.

Separately, heat 4 tbsp ghee, add ladies fingers and fry for about 8 minutes. When meat is tender and gravy of a thick consistency add ladies fingers together with tomatoes. Stir and remove from heat. Garnish with green peas.

Salad with Peanut Sauce Dressing

Bamiah

Stuffed Beef Roll

Indian Mutton Soup

MEE SOTO

Ingredients:

- [ ] 1 chicken *weighing about 1.75 kg*
- [ ] 6 cups water
- [ ] salt to taste
- [ ] 600 g fresh yellow noodles
- [ ] 300 g bean sprouts - *remove tails*

Grind into a fine paste:

- [ ] $1^1/_2$ tbsp coriander (ketumbar) *seeds*
- [ ] 1 tsp cumin (jintan puteh) *seeds*
- [ ] 1 tsp fennel (jintan manis) *seeds*
- [ ] 1 stalk lemon grass (serai) - *slice*
- [ ] 1 thick slice lengkuas
- [ ] 4 candlenuts (buah keras)
- [ ] 8-10 shallots
- [ ] 1 tsp white peppercorns

For garnishing:

- [ ] 10 shallots - *cut into fine slices and fry till golden brown*
- [ ] spring onions and celery - *chop fine*
- [ ] potato cutlets - *fry*
- [ ] shredded chicken

Chilli Padi Sauce:

- [ ] $^1/_4$ cup birds-eye chilli (chilli padi) - *wash and remove stalks; grind fine and pour some dark soya sauce over it.*

Method:

Put whole chicken, ground paste, water and salt in a large pot. Bring to the boil. When boiling, remove chicken and keep stock aside to use as soup for the Mee Soto.

Put the chicken on a tray and roast for about 20 – 30 minutes at 190°C (375°F) until a light brown. Shred chicken when cool.

Bring a large pan of water to the boil. When water is actively boiling, put in noodles and bring back to the boil. Continue boiling till noodles are cooked, then remove noodles.

In the same water, scald the bean sprouts.

To serve:

Put the noodles in a dish, sprinkle bean sprouts and shredded chicken over it then add soup and garnishing. Serve with Chilli Padi Sauce.

FRIED KWEI TEOW

Ingredients:

- [ ] 600g fresh flat rice flour noodles (kwei teow)
- [ ] 120g beef - *thinly sliced*
- [ ] 300g shrimps - *peel*
- [ ] 20 fish balls - *cut in half*
- [ ] 300g spring greens (chye sim) - *cut into 5cm (2in) lengths*
- [ ] 8 shallots ⎫ *Grind coarsely:*
- [ ] 2 small cloves garlic ⎭
- [ ] 2 tsp cornflour ⎫
- [ ] 3 tbsp light soya sauce ⎪
- [ ] 1 tsp pepper ⎬ *Mix together:*
- [ ] 1 cup water ⎭
- [ ] 6 tbsp oil
- [ ] salt to taste

Method:

Heat oil, add ground ingredients and fry till fragrant. Add beef, shrimps, fish balls, chye sim and salt, stir frying after each addition. Add cornflour mixture. When bubbling, add kwei teow and stir, mixing all ingredients well. Serve immediately.

Mee Siam Lemak

Mee Soto

Fried Kwei Teow

MEE SIAM LEMAK

Ingredients:

- [ ] 80 g salted ikan kurau (or dried salt cod)
- [ ] 4 pieces hard beancurd (taukwa) - cut each into small cubes and rub with salt
- [ ] 25 dried chillies - cut and soak
- [ ] 10 shallots
- [ ] 1 clove garlic
- [ ] 2 tbsp salted soyabeans (taucheo)
- [ ] 300 g thick dried rice noodles (beehoon kasar) - soak for about 1 - 2 hours then cut into shorter lengths
- [ ] 300 g shrimps - remove shell
- [ ] cooked coconut crumbs made from milk of $^1/_2$ coconut (see recipe for coconut crumbs)
- [ ] 300 g bean sprouts - remove tails
- [ ] salt to taste
- [ ] 12 tbsp oil
- [ ] 4 hard boiled eggs - sliced ⎫
- [ ] a bunch of coarse chives (kuchai) ⎬ for garnishing
    - cut into 3 cm ($1^1/_4$ in) lengths
- [ ] a few small limes- cut into half ⎭

Method:

Roast the pieces of ikan kurau in a dry , hot pan until fish is slightly brown. Remove from heat, flake it then grind into a fine paste with chillies, shallots, garlic and taucheo.

Heat oil, fry taukwa cubes till slightly brown, then put aside in a dish. In the same oil, fry the ground ingredients, adding salt, till fragrant. Add shrimps, stir fry for a few minutes then add coconut crumbs. Stir, add noodles and stir fry, mixing the noodles with other ingredients. Add bean sprouts, mix and stir fry for a few more minutes then remove from heat. Garnish with fried taukwa, sliced hard boiled eggs, kuchai and limes.

COOKED COCONUT CRUMBS

These cooked crumbs are used for garnishing Mee Siam Lemak and for Ikan Bilis Sambal.

Ingredients:

- [ ] 450g grated coconut - add 2 cups water and extract equal amount of milk

Method:

Put the coconut milk into a pan and boil over low heat. When liquid has been absorbed and all that remains is oil and crumbly coconut, keep stirring. When the coconut crumbs are brown, remove from pan.

The crumbs can be stored in an air tight jar.

DRY CHAP CHYE

Ingredients:

- [ ] 300g shrimps - peel
- [ ] 2 hard beancurd (taukwa) - deep fry lightly and cut each into 9 squares
- [ ] 60g beancurd stick (fu chok) - cut into 5-6cm (2-2 $^1/_2$ in) lengths and soak to soften
- [ ] 40g dried lily buds(kim chiam) - soak and remove tiny hard portion at one end of stalk. Tie into a knot.
- [ ] 20g dried mushrooms - soak in hot water then cut off stems and cut each mushroom in half
- [ ] 40g dried beancurd sheets (tim chok) - soak and cut into fine strips
- [ ] 20g black fungus (telinga tikus) - soak
- [ ] 2 small bundles bean thread vermicelli (sohoon) - soak
- [ ] 300g cabbage - cut into pieces
- [ ] $^1/_2$ cup oil
- [ ] 3 tbsp salted soya beans (taucheo) ⎫
- [ ] 2 cloves garlic ⎬ Grind coarsely
- [ ] 10 shallots ⎭
- [ ] 6 tbsp oil
- [ ] 2 tbsp light soya sauce

Method:

Heat about $^1/_2$ cup of oil and fry each of the above items separately, except for sohoon and shrimps, and keep aside. They are to be only lightly browned. Heat 6 tbsp oil, fry ground ingredients till fragrant. Add shrimps, fry, add soya sauce and all the fried ingredients except cabbage and stir fry. Add cabbage, then sohoon, stirring after each addition, and stir fry for a few more minutes before removing from heat.

FRIED POH PIAH
(Spring Rolls)

Ingredients:

- [ ] **2 tbsp salted soya beans (taucheo)**
- [ ] **1 clove garlic** } *Grind coursely*
- [ ] **2 tbsp oil**
- [ ] **$^{1}/_{2}$ cup water**
- [ ] **150g small shrimps** - *remove shell*
- [ ] **100g crab meat**
- [ ] **150g bamboo shoot** - *shred (canned bamboo shoots may be used)*
- [ ] **75g yam bean (bangkwang)** - *shred*
- [ ] **150g bean sprouts** - *remove tails*
- [ ] **2 pcs hard bean curd (taukwa)** - *cut into small squares and deep fry*
- [ ] **a few stalks big coriander leaves** - *cut into 1cm ($^{1}/_{2}$ in) lengths*
- [ ] **200g spring roll pastry (poh piah skin)** - *125 mm square sheets*

Method:

Heat oil, add ground taucheo-garlic paste and stir fry for a minute then add water and continue to fry till fragrant.

Add shrimps and crab meat, fry for a few minutes, then add bamboo shoot, bankwang and bean sprouts, stirring after each addition for a few minutes. Remove from heat and sprinkle fried taukwa over it. Leave to cool.

To wrap:

Put about a tablespoon of cooked filling on each skin, add one or two pieces of coriander leaves and wrap to form a roll. Seal the ends with a flour-water paste.

Heat sufficient oil for deep frying and fry rolls till golden brown.

Serve with chilli sauce. Garnish with tomato and cucumber slices

Note: Frozen spring roll pastry is available in supermarkets.

GINGER PICKLE

Ingredients:

- [ ] **150g young ginger** - *peel and slice paper thin*
- [ ] **3 tbsp granulated sugar**
- [ ] **$^{1}/_{2}$ cup vinegar**

Method:

Either mix all ingredients and leave to stand for at least one day before using, or boil vinegar and sugar, cool then add ginger slices.

Store in a glass jar.

Serve with century egg.

HONEYDEW FRIED CHICKEN

Ingredients:
- [ ] *1 chicken weighing about 1.5 kg - cut into average size pieces*
- [ ] *1 tsp pepper*
- [ ] *2 tbsp dark soya sauce*
- [ ] *oil for deep frying*
- [ ] *120g cashew nuts*

Method:

Combine chicken with pepper, honey and soya sauce and leave to marinate for 1 hour. Drain chicken. Heat oil and deep fry chicken till golden brown.

Deep fry cashew nuts till golden brown. When serving, sprinkle cashew nuts over chicken and garnish with slices of cucumber. Serve hot.

Honeydew Fried Chicken

Dry Chap Chye

Century Egg with Ginger Pickle

Fried Poh Piah

37

Ikan Belada

Spicy Long Beans

Fish Head Soup with Black Pepper

IKAN BELADA

Ingredients:

- [ ] 1 ikan kledek (about 500g) - *make 2 slashes on each side of fish*
- [ ] 1 large turmeric leaf (daun kunyit) - *wash well*
- [ ] 1 rectangular piece banana leaf - *scald to soften*
- [ ] 10 red chillies
- [ ] 4 shallots
- [ ] 2 cloves garlic
- [ ] 2 stalks lemon grass (serai) — *cut up into pieces then grind (not too fine)*
- [ ] 1 pc lengkuas (size of walnut)
- [ ] 1cm piece fresh turmeric
- [ ] 3 tbsp oil
- [ ] 1 heaped tsp brown sugar
- [ ] salt to taste
- [ ] 3-4 stalks daun kesom (optional) - *wash leaves, shake dry and shred*
- [ ] 1 heaped tbsp tamarind pulp
- [ ] 2 tbsp water — *mix and strain to obtain tamarind juice*

Method:

Heat oil, add ground ingredients and fry till fragrant. Add sugar, salt and tamarind juice. Boil till thick.

Put turmeric leaf in center of banana leaf. Spoon half the cooked chilli mixture and shredded daun kesom (if used) on to turmeric leaf. Spread mixture on leaf. Put fish over this. Spread rest of chilli mixture over fish, sprinkle daun kesom.

Fold the two long sides of the banana leaf over fish so they overlap. Skewer ends with strong toothpick. Grill for 25-30 minutes.

Alternatively, barbecue the fish.

Serve with Spicy Long Beans.

SPICY LONG BEANS

Ingredients:

- [ ] 150g long beans - *cut into 4cm lengths*
- [ ] 2 red chillies
- [ ] 4 shallots
- [ ] 1 clove garlic — *grind to a paste*
- [ ] 1 tsp dried silver fish (fine ikan bilis) - *soak till soft*
- [ ] 2 tbsp oil
- [ ] salt to taste
- [ ] a pinch of turmeric powder

Method:

Heat oil, add chilli paste, fry till fragrant. Add long beans, salt and turmeric powder. Stir well. Do not overcook beans.

FISH HEAD SOUP WITH BLACK PEPPER

Ingredients:

- [ ] 1 fish head - *sea bream or threadfin (ikan kerisi or ikan kurau) approximately 1kg in weight*
- [ ] 1 tsp black peppercorns - *grind coarse*

Ingredients for frying:

- [ ] 3 shallots
- [ ] 1 red chilli
- [ ] 1cm slice ginger — *chop fine*
- [ ] 2 cloves garlic
- [ ] 1 stalk spring onion - *cut into 1cm length*
- [ ] 1 stalk coriander leaves - *chop coarsely*
- [ ] 4 cups water
- [ ] salt to taste
- [ ] 2 heaped tbsp black fungus - *soak, clean, remove hard stumps and drain*
- [ ] 1/2 bundle bean thread vermicelli (sohoon) - *soak and cut into shorter lengths*
- [ ] 2 tomatoes - *cut into wedges*
- [ ] 2 tbsp oil

Method:

Cut fish head into large pieces, wash well and rub with black pepper. Heat oil, add ingredients for frying. When fragrant, add spring onion and coriander leaves. Stir then add water, salt, black fungus and vermicelli. When water is boiling, add fish head, cover pot and simmer. When almost cooked, add tomato wedges.

Malaysian & Indonesian Dishes

NASI AMBANG

Ingredients:
- [ ] 600g rice - soak in water for 4 to 5 hours then drain
- [ ] 2 fragrant screwpine leaves (daun pandan) - wash and tie into a bundle
- [ ] 2 $^1/_2$ cups water

Method:
Boil water in steamer.

Put rice, pandan leaves and 2 $^1/_2$ cups water in a deep tray and steam till rice is cooked.

IKAN GORENG

Ingredients:
- [ ] 4 small pieces ikan tenggiri (Spanish mackerel or bonito) - wash and dry
- [ ] 1 tsp turmeric powder
- [ ] salt to taste
- [ ] 2 tsp water
- [ ] oil for shallow frying

Method:
Mix turmeric powder, salt and water into a thick paste.

Rub the pieces of fish evenly with paste and fry in oil till golden brown.

FRIED OX LUNG

Ingredients:
- [ ] 250g ox lung
- [ ] 1 tbsp turmeric powder
- [ ] $^1/_2$ tbsp coriander powder } mix
- [ ] salt to taste
- [ ] oil for deep frying

Method:
Put ox lung in saucepan with enough water to cover it and half teaspoon salt. Boil till tender. Remove and cut into $^1/_2$cm thick slices.

Marinate slices with a mixture of turmeric and coriander powder and salt.

Heat oil. Add ox lung slices and fry till a little brown.

Urap Taugeh

Sambal Goreng

Chicken Curry (Indonesian Style)

Potato Cutlet

Rendang Rempah

Ikan Goreng

Nasi Ambang   Serundeng

Fried Ox Lung

Tempe

Sambal Terong

41

CHICKEN CURRY
(Indonesian Style)

Ingredients:
- [ ] 1 chicken weighing about 1.8 kg - cut into large pieces

Grind to a fine powder:
- [ ] 1¹/₂ tsp peppercorns
- [ ] 3 slightly heaped tbsp coriander (ketumbar) seeds
      - roast in dry pan before grinding

- [ ] 12-15 shallots - peel
- [ ] 3 red chillies } grind to a smooth paste
- [ ] 2 cloves garlic
- [ ] 6 thin slices ginger
- [ ] 1 stalk lemon grass (serai) } bruise
- [ ] 1 piece lengkuas (size of walnut)
- [ ] ¹/₄ tsp turmeric powder
- [ ] salt to taste
- [ ] 230g grated coconut - mix with 2 cups water and extract
      equal amount of milk
- [ ] 1 cup water
- [ ] 8 tbsp oil

Method:
In a large bowl, combine chicken with all the ground ingredients, *serai*, *lengkuas*, turmeric powder, and salt.

Heat oil, add chicken and fry till fragrant. Add water and coconut milk, then cover and bring to the boil. Simmer till chicken is tender, stirring now and then during cooking. The consistency of the gravy should be thick.

URAP TAUGEH
(Bean Sprouts with Grated Coconut)

Ingredients:
- [ ] 300g bean sprouts (taugeh) - remove tails, wash and drain
- [ ] 1 cup grated coconut
- [ ] salt to taste
- [ ] 2 limes - extract juice
- [ ] 10 dried chillies - soak in water to soften } grind to a
- [ ] 5 shallots   fine paste
- [ ] 15 dried prawns - soak, wash and drain

Method:
Place a shallow frying pan over low heat.

Put grated coconut into the dry frying pan and add the ground ingredients and salt. Keep on stirring until fragrant. Add bean sprouts and stir for 1-2 minutes only. Do not overcook the bean sprouts.

Remove from fire and sprinkle lime juice over the bean sprouts. Mix before putting in serving dish.

SERUNDENG
(Spiced Grated Coconut)

Ingredients:
- [ ] 1 cup grated coconut (with skin)
- [ ] ¹/₂ teacup tamarind juice - made with 2 tsp tamarind
- [ ] 1 tbsp sugar
- [ ] 1 tsp salt
- [ ] 2 fragrant lime leaves (daun limau perut)
- [ ] 1 tbsp meat curry powder

Grind into a smooth paste:
- [ ] 3-4 shallots
- [ ] 1 stalk lemon grass (serai)
- [ ] 1 small piece lengkuas (1cm or ¹/₂ in thick)
- [ ] 1 small clove garlic

Method:
Put the grated coconut in a shallow saucepan and add ground ingredients, curry powder, tamarind juice, sugar, lime leaves and salt. Mix well and cook over low heat, turning the contents over from time to time to prevent burning, until dry and crumbly.

TEMPE
(Fermented Soya Bean Cake)

Ingredients:
- [ ] 2 packets fermented soya bean cake (tempe) - use whole
- [ ] 1 tsp turmeric powder
- [ ] salt to taste
- [ ] 2 tsp water
- [ ] oil for deep frying

Method:
Mix salt, turmeric powder and water into a paste and rub it into the pieces of *tempe*.

Heat oil and fry *tempe* till brown.

Note: Tempe is available in markets

RENDANG REMPAH

Ingredients:

- [ ] 600g beef or mutton - *cut into small pieces*
- [ ] 4 level tbsp coriander (ketumbar) *powder*
- [ ] $^1/_2$ tbsp cumin (jintan puteh) *powder*
- [ ] 1 stalk lemon grass (serai) - *bruise*
- [ ] 1 piece lengkuas *the size of a walnut* - *bruise*
- [ ] 2 fragrant lime leaves (daun limau perut)
- [ ] 1 small turmeric leaf - *use whole*
- [ ] 450g grated coconut - *set aside 2 tbsp to be roasted over low heat till brown. Add 5 cups water and extract 6 cups thick milk from the rest of the coconut*
- [ ] 2 tsp sugar
- [ ] salt to taste

Grind into a smooth paste:

- [ ] 10 dried chillies - *remove seeds for a mild flavour and soak in hot water to soften*
- [ ] 8 shallots
- [ ] 2 tbsp roasted coconut taken from allowance

Method:

Combine ground ingredients with meat in a deep pan. Add coconut milk, turmeric leaf, lime leaves, *serai*, *lengkuas*, coriander powder, cumin powder, sugar and salt. Bring to the boil and continue to cook uncovered till meat is tender, then reduce heat and cook till quite dry, turning over the contents from time to time to prevent burning.

POTATO CUTLETS

Ingredients:

- [ ] 2 large potatoes - *peel and cut into thick slices*
- [ ] 5-6 shallots - *slice thinly*
- [ ] 2 spring onions - *chop finely*
- [ ] $^1/_2$ tsp pepper
- [ ] salt to taste
- [ ] 1 egg - *beat lightly*
- [ ] oil for deep frying

Method:

Heat oil in frying pan and fry potatoes till golden brown, then put in a bowl. Fry shallots till brown and add to the potatoes. While potatoes are still warm, add pepper, spring onions and salt and mash till smooth. Shape into small ovals or rounds and coat with beaten egg. Deep fry till golden brown.

SAMBAL GORENG

Ingredients:

- [ ] 300g ox liver - *cut into small squares*
- [ ] 300g shrimps - *remove shells and tails*
- [ ] 6 tbsp oil
- [ ] 1 tbsp sugar
- [ ] salt to taste
- [ ] 1 big onion
- [ ] 2 red chillies } *thinly sliced*
- [ ] 1 green chilli
- [ ] $1^1/_2$ cups thick coconut milk - *extracted from 230g grated coconut mixed with 1 cup water*
- [ ] 1 stalk lemon grass (serai) - *bruise*
- [ ] 1 small piece lengkuas - *bruise*
- [ ] $^1/_2$ teacup light tamarind juice - *made with 2 tsp tamarind*
- [ ] 10 dried chillies - *soak to soften and remove seeds for a mild flavour*
- [ ] 2 candlenuts (buah keras)
- [ ] 1 tsp dried shrimp paste (blacan)
- [ ] 6-8 shallots

} *grind to a smooth paste*

Method:

Heat oil in deep frying pan and fry ground ingredients together with *serai* and *lengkuas*. Add salt and sugar and fry till fragrant then add liver and shrimps. Stir fry, mixing evenly with the fried paste, for a few minutes, then add thick coconut milk together with tamarind juice. Reduce heat and leave to simmer till gravy is fairly thick. Add sliced chillies and onions and cook till almost dry.

SAMBAL TERONG

Ingredients:

- [ ] 2 green eggplant (brinjal or terong) - *cut into half, season with salt and leave for 5 minutes*
- [ ] 8 fresh chillies
- [ ] 1 piece dried shrimp paste (blacan) (5cm x 2.5cm or 2in x 1in) - *flatten to make a patty and roast over low heat till brown*
- [ ] 1 tsp sugar
- [ ] salt to taste

Method:

Grill *brinjal* for 10-12 minutes till flesh is soft. Scrape flesh from the skin with a spoon and put in a bowl.

Discard skin.

Grind chillies and *blacan* and add to brinjal pulp together with sugar and salt, and mix well.

SARDINE SALAD

Ingredients:

- [ ] 1 can local sardines (15oz or 425g) - see glossary
- [ ] ¹/₂ cucumber - peel
- [ ] ¹/₄ pineapple } cut into small squares
- [ ] 2 medium sized tomatoes
- [ ] 1 big onion - chop
- [ ] 2 red chillies } slice
- [ ] 1 green chilli
- [ ] pinch of salt
- [ ] pepper
- [ ] some small coriander leaves for garnishing - chop

Method:

Arrange sardines on a platter. Mix all the other ingredients together and spread over sardines. Sprinkle with coriander leaves before serving.

YOUNG CORN AND MUSHROOM IN COCONUT MILK

Ingredients:

- [ ] 1 can (225g) young corn - use whole
- [ ] 1 small can (198g) button mushroom
- [ ] 300g shrimps - peel
- [ ] 6 shallots
- [ ] 3 candlenuts (buah keras)
- [ ] 1 piece fresh turmeric - (1cm or ¹/₂ in cube) } grind to a fine paste
- [ ] 3 red chillies
- [ ] 4 tbsp oil
- [ ] 230g grated coconut - add 1¹/₂ cups water and extract equal amount of milk
- [ ] salt to taste
- [ ] 20 birds-eye chilli (chilli padi)

Method:

Heat oil, fry ground ingredients till fragrant. Add corn and mushroom, stir for a minute, then add coconut milk and salt and bring to the boil. Add *chilli padi*, leave to boil for a little longer then add shrimps and continue to boil, stirring all the time, for another 10 minutes.

Note: Add 2-3 sardines (from a can) at the end, heat through and serve.
This is optional.

SAMBAL SARDINE WITH GREEN MANGO

Ingredients:

- [ ] 1 can local sardines (15oz or 425g) - see glossary
- [ ] 12-15 dried chillies - soak beforehand
- [ ] 10 shallots
- [ ] 1 thin slice ginger } grind to a smooth paste
- [ ] 1 clove garlic
- [ ] 4 candlenuts (buah keras)
- [ ] 3 tbsp oil
- [ ] 2 green mangos - peel, cut into half. Remove seed and cut each half into 4.
- [ ] 2 large onions - cut into thick slices
- [ ] salt to taste

Method:

Heat oil, add ground ingredients and salt and fry till fragrant. Add sardines (include sauce, if any) and stir, mixing well with paste. After a minute or two, add onions and mango, stir fry for about 1 minute then remove from heat.

Note: Replace mango with 10-12 blimbing if available. Cut blimbing in half lengthwise.

SARDINE WITH PINEAPPLE IN COCONUT MILK

Ingredients:

- [ ] 1 can local sardines (15oz or 425g) - see glossary
- [ ] 10 dried chillies - soak to soften
- [ ] 1 clove garlic
- [ ] 1 piece ginger - size of almond
- [ ] big onion } grind to a smooth paste
- [ ] 1 cm (¹/₂ in) cube fresh turmeric
- [ ] 1 stalk lemon grass (serai) - bruise
- [ ] ¹/₂ small pineapple - cut into small wedges
- [ ] 230g grated coconut - add 1¹/₂ cups water and extract equal amount of milk
- [ ] salt to taste
- [ ] 5 tbsp oil

Method:

Heat oil, add ground ingredients and lemon grass and fry till fragrant. Add pineapple, coconut milk and salt and bring to the boil, stirring now and then. When boiling, add sardines and leave to cook for 5 mins.

Sambal Sardine with Mango

*Young Corn and Mushroom
in Coconut Milk*

Sardine with Pineapple in Coconut Milk

*Sardine
Salad*

45

Sayur Kangkong Keledek

Asam Pedas Melaka

Gulai Nanas

Sambal Mangga

46

SAMBAL MANGGA

Ingredients:

- [ ] *2 medium size green mango - wash well and cut into small cubes (do not peel)*
- [ ] *2 green chillies* ⎫
- [ ] *2 red chillies* ⎬ *cut into small pieces*
- [ ] *10 chilli padi - use whole*
- [ ] *1 tbsp sugar* ⎫
- [ ] *2 tbsp dark soya sauce* ⎬ *mix*
- [ ] *salt to taste* ⎭

Method:

Put mango and chillies in a dish. Pour soya sauce mixture over this and mix well

ASAM PEDAS MELAKA
(Kuah Lada)

Ingredients:

- [ ] *1 tbsp coriander (ketumbar) seeds* ⎫
- [ ] *$^1/_2$ tsp cumin (jintan puteh) seeds* ⎬ *roast in dry pan*
- [ ] *$^1/_2$ tsp fennel (jintan manis) seeds* ⎭
- [ ] *1 piece fresh turmeric (size of almond)*
- [ ] *25 dried chillies - soak*
- [ ] *1 tbsp dried shrimp paste (blacan)*
- [ ] *2 tbsp grated coconut - roast in dry pan over low heat*
- [ ] *2 cloves garlic*
- [ ] *1 small piece ginger (size of almond)*
- [ ] *1 onion*
- [ ] *600g ikan tenggiri (Spanish mackerel or bonito) - cut into 6-8 pieces about 1cm ($^1/_2$in) thick; rub with salt then wash*
- [ ] *$^1/_4$ medium sized cabbage - cut into 5 wedge-like slices; cut off hard stem*
- [ ] *10 tbsp oil*
- [ ] *$1^1/_2$ tbsp tamarind - add 3 cups water, mix and strain to get tamarind juice*
- [ ] *salt to taste*

Method:

Grind the following ingredients starting with coriander then cumin, fennel, turmeric, chillies, *blacan*, coconut, garlic, ginger and onion, adding each ingredient only when the previous one is finely ground.

Heat oil, add ground ingredients and fry till fragrant. Add salt and tamarind juice, stir, then add fish. Cover and bring to the boil then add cabbage slices. As soon as cabbage is cooked, remove from heat. Do not overcook cabbage

SAYUR KANGKONG KELEDEK
(Water Convolvulus and Sweet Potato in Coconut Gravy)

Ingredients:

- [ ] *450g grated coconut - mix with 4 cups water and extract equal amount of milk*
- [ ] *300g sweet potatoes - peel and cut into medium sized pieces*
- [ ] *salt to taste*
- [ ] *120g shrimps - peel*
- [ ] *600g kangkong (water convolvulus) - wash and cut into 5cm (2in) lengths; discard fibrous end of stalk*

Pound or grind fine:
- [ ] *2 red chillies*
- [ ] *6-9 shallots*
- [ ] *$^1/_2$ tsp dried shrimp paste (blacan)*

Method:

In a pot, combine ground ingredients with 3 cups coconut milk, salt and sweet potatoes. Bring to the boil; when coconut milk is about to boil, keep stirring to prevent it from curdling.

When potatoes are a little soft, add shrimps, *kangkong* and the remaining cup of coconut milk. Bring to the boil, stirring all the time, then cook for 5 minutes before removing from heat.

SAMBAL BLACAN

Ingredients:

- [ ] *1 piece dried shrimp paste (blacan) - 2x2.5 x1 cm or ($^3/_4$ x1 x$^1/_2$ in) - roast in a dry pan*
- [ ] *8 fresh red chillies - cut each in three*
- [ ] *salt to taste*
- [ ] *2 small limes (limau kesturi)*

Method:

Put salt in pounder with a couple of chillies and pound, gradually add more chillies till all are used up. Finally, add blacan and continue to pound.

The final mixture should be neither too fine nor too coarse.

Squeeze lime juice over paste when serving.

GULAI NANAS

Ingredients:
- ☐ 2 tbsp oil
- ☐ 10 dried chillies - soak
- ☐ 1 piece dried shrimp paste (blacan)
  - 2 x 2 x 0.5 cm ($^3/_4$ x $^3/_4$ x $^1/_4$ in)
- ☐ 8 shallots
- ☐ 1 piece fresh turmeric
  - about 2cm ($^3/_4$ in) long

  } grind to a fine paste
- ☐ 1 stalk lemon grass (serai)
- ☐ 1 small piece lengkuas

  } bruise
- ☐ 1 tsp salt
- ☐ 1 tbsp sugar
- ☐ $^1/_2$ almost-ripe pineapple - cut into two pieces lengthwise and then cut each piece into wedges about 1 cm ($^1/_2$ in) thick
- ☐ 2 cups water
- ☐ 1 tsp tamarind - mix with $^1/_2$ teacup water and extract juice
- ☐ 5 pieces ikan tenggiri (Spanish mackerel or bonito)

Method:
Heat oil in a pot and fry the ground ingredients, *serai* and *lengkuas* till fragrant. Add salt, sugar, pineapple and water. Cover pot and boil for 3-5 minutes. Add tamarind juice and *ikan tenggiri*, cover and boil a few minutes over low heat. As soon as fish is cooked, remove from heat.

SAMBAL SOTONG KERING

Ingredients:
- ☐ 2 large pieces dried cuttlefish (sotong) - cut into small pieces and soak in water for 1-2 hours
- ☐ 1 tbsp tamarind - add $^1/_2$ cup water and extract $^1/_2$ cup juice
- ☐ 1 tbsp sugar
- ☐ salt to taste
- ☐ 5 tbsp oil

Grind to a fine paste:
- ☐ 20 dried chillies - soak and seed
- ☐ 2 medium sized onions
- ☐ 1 piece dried shrimp paste (blacan) (2.5cm or 1in square)

Method:
Heat oil, add ground ingredients, salt and sugar, and fry till fragrant. Add *sotong*, fry for a while then add tamarind juice and leave to cook till fairly dry.

BITTER GOURD WITH TAUKWA

Ingredients:
- ☐ 1 large bitter gourd - cut in half then cut each half into slices about 0.5cm ($^1/_4$ in) thick; sprinkle with salt and let stand for about 15 mins; wash
- ☐ 300g shrimps - peel
- ☐ 2 large pieces hard beancurd (taukwa) - cut into squares and deep fry
- ☐ 1 cup grated coconut - add 1 cup water and extract 1 cup milk
- ☐ salt to taste
- ☐ 4 tbsp oil
- ☐ 10 dried chillies - soak to soften
- ☐ 1 medium sized onion
- ☐ 1 clove garlic

  } grind to a fine paste

Method:
Heat oil, add ground ingredients and salt and fry till fragrant. Add shrimps and fry for a few minutes. Add *taukwa* and coconut milk, and bring to the boil. When gravy thickens, add bitter gourd and cook till fairly dry, stirring now and then.

Bitter Gourd with Taukwa

Ikan Masak Kuning

Sambal Sotong Kering

49

Ikan Masak Kuning

Ingredients:
- ☐ 1 small ikan tenggiri *(Spanish mackerel or bonito)* - cut into about eight pieces
- ☐ 230g grated coconut - add 2 cups water and extract 2 cups milk
- ☐ 1 stalk lemon grass (serai) - bruised
- ☐ 20 birds-eye chillies (chilli padi)
- ☐ 10-12 blimbing - cut in half
- ☐ salt to taste
- ☐ 1 piece fresh turmeric - size of almond ⎫
- ☐ 8 shallots ⎬ grind to a fine paste
- ☐ 4 dried chillies - soak to soften ⎭

Method:
Put coconut milk, fish, *serai*, ground ingredients, salt and *chilli padi* in a cooking pot. Put over low heat and bring to the boil slowly, stirring now and then. Add blimbing and boil for 5 minutes.

Papaya With Shellfish

Ingredients:
- ☐ 600g cockles or clams (kerang) - scrub thoroughly
- ☐ 2 tsp dried silver fish
- ☐ 1/2 tsp black peppercorns ⎫
- ☐ 5 shallots ⎬ grind fine
- ☐ salt to taste
- ☐ 1 small unripe papaya (about 450g) - peel and cut into slices
- ☐ 2 1/2 cups water

Method:
Put all the above ingredients in a pot. Bring to the boil. Boil for about 5 minutes before removing from heat.

Ikan Bawal Cuka

Ingredients:
- ☐ salt to taste
- ☐ 1/2 tbsp sugar
- ☐ 1 tbsp vinegar
- ☐ 100 ml water
- ☐ 8 tbsp oil
- ☐ 1 ikan bawal *(black pomfret, flounder or John Dory)* weighing about 900g - clean well, make two slashes on each side of the fish and rub with salt.
- ☐ 2 red chillies ⎫
- ☐ 2 green chillies ⎬ cut each into two lengthwise
- ☐ 2 big onions - slice rather thick
- ☐ 6 medium sized tomatoes - slice rather thick
- ☐ 10 red chillies ⎫
- ☐ 1 onion ⎪
- ☐ 1 clove garlic ⎬ grind to a fine paste
- ☐ 6 candle nuts (buah keras) ⎭

Method:
Deep fry fish till brown, then put aside on a dish. Heat 8 tablespoons oil and fry ground ingredients till fragrant. Add salt, sugar, vinegar and cook for a while. Add water, tomatoes, onions and chillies. Cook for a few minutes then pour over fish.

Steamed Ikan Bilis Fritters

Sambal Cuka

Opor Sotong

Papaya with Shellfish

Ikan Bawal Cuka

STEAMED IKAN BILIS FRITTERS

Ingredients:

- [ ] 230g plain flour
- [ ] 120g rice flour
- [ ] 150g steamed silver fish (ikan bilis)
- [ ] 3 eggs
- [ ] 2 tsp coriander (ketumbar seeds) } roast then grind
- [ ] $^1/_4$ tsp cumin (jintan puteh) } coarsely
- [ ] 1 small bunch big coriander leaves - chop fine
- [ ] salt to taste
- [ ] 200 ml water
- [ ] oil for deep frying

Method:

Put the two types of flour, ground spices and salt in a bowl. Break eggs into flour, add coriander leaves and water, stir and mix well.

Add fish and mix.

Heat oil then drop mixture by the spoonful into oil using a dessertspoon. Fry till golden brown.

Serve with *Sambal Cuka*.

OPOR SOTONG

Ingredients:

- [ ] 4 tbsp oil
- [ ] 1 clove garlic
- [ ] 1 medium sized onion
- [ ] 1 piece fresh turmeric - about 0.5cm (¹/₄ in) long — grind to a smooth paste
- [ ] 12 dried chillies - soak
- [ ] 2 tbsp coriander (ketumbar) powder
- [ ] 1 tsp cumin (jintan puteh) powder — add to ground ingredients
- [ ] 1 stalk lemon grass (serai)
- [ ] 1 piece lengkuas - 1cm (¹/₂ thick) — bruise
- [ ] 450g grated coconut (put aside 2 tbsp for roasting) - add 2 cups water and extract 3 cups milk
- [ ] salt to taste
- [ ] 2 fragrant lime leaves (daun limau purut)
- [ ] 600g medium or big squid (sotong) - separate head from body, remove bag of fluid, wash and drain

Method:

Heat oil in pot and fry ground ingredients together with *serai*, *lengkuas*, roasted coconut, salt and lime leaves till fragrant. Add coconut milk. When boiling, stir, reduce heat and simmer until gravy becomes thick, stirring occasionally. Add *sotong* and cook for 5 minutes. Do not overcook as *sotong* will become rubbery.

SAMBAL CUKA

Ingredients:

- [ ] 10 red chillies
- [ ] 1 thick slice ginger (about 1 cm or ¹/₂ in thick)
- [ ] 1 clove garlic
- [ ] 2 tbsp vinegar
- [ ] 1 tbsp sugar (slightly heaped)
- [ ] 1 tsp salt

Method:

Pound chillies, ginger and garlic until fine, then put in a bowl and mix with vinegar, salt and sugar.

STEAMED NASI UDUK

Ingredients:

- [ ] 600g rice - wash and soak overnight in water to which a teaspoon of salt has been added
- [ ] 450g grated coconut - remove skin before grating; add 3¹/₂ cups water and extract an equal amount of milk
- [ ] 3-4 fragrant screwpine leaves (daun pandan)

Method:

Boil water in steamer. Drain rice, put in a steaming tray, pour 2 cups coconut milk and break *pandan* leaves over it. Steam for 15-20 minutes, then uncover, stir rice, add 1¹/₂ cups coconut milk, stir and continue steaming. After 15 minutes, stir rice again and continue cooking for another 15 minutes.

Sufficient for 6-8 people.

Note: To serve, put the cooked Nasi Uduk on a platter, sprinkle shredded omelette over it and garnish with cucumber slices. If making little omelettes, cut each in half and arrange them around the platter of rice.

OTAK-OTAK
(Steamed Spicy Fish in Banana Leaves)

Ingredients:

- [ ] 450g ikan tenggiri (Spanish mackerel or bonito) - buy tail end
- [ ] 1 stalk lemon grass (serai)
- [ ] 1 piece lengkuas (size of walnut)
- [ ] 10 shallots — pound or grind
- [ ] 3 heaped tbsp grated coconut
- [ ] salt to taste
- [ ] 3 heaped tbsp fish curry powder - mix with sufficient water to form a paste
- [ ] 5 rectangular pieces banana leaves - each measuring 25 x 15 cm (10 x 6in)

Method:

Clean fish, remove scales then fillet the fish. Using a spoon, scrape off meat and chop.

Combine ground ingredients and salt with curry paste then add fish and mix well.

Put 2 tablespoons of mixture in centre of banana leaf and fold, bringing the two long edges towards the centre so that they overlap. Secure ends with toothpicks. Steam for about ¹/₂ hour.

Makes about 5.

Note: The skin and bones of the fish can be used for making fish stock.

OMELETTE

Ingredients:

- ☐ 4 eggs
- ☐ 1 big onion - *chop*
- ☐ 1-2 red chillies - *slice*
- ☐ 1 spring onion
- ☐ 2 stalks coriander leaves } *chop*
- ☐ ¹/₂ *tsp pepper*
- ☐ *salt to taste*
- ☐ 1 tbsp oil

Method:

Break eggs into bowl, beat, add chopped and sliced ingredients, pepper and salt and mix well.

Heat oil. Pour half the egg mixture into pan and fry over moderate heat, first one side then the other. Repeat, using up mixture.

Alternative Method:

Heat oil. Pour egg mixture into rings for poached eggs to make little omelettes.

Otak-Otak

Omelette

Fried Kangkong
with Blacan

Steamed Nasi Uduk

Sambal
Prawns

Ayam Panggang
Gahru

SAMBAL PRAWNS

Ingredients:

- ☐ 600g prawns - *peel and devein*
- ☐ 1 tbsp tamarind - *mix with 4 tbsp water and strain to get juice*
- ☐ ¹/₂ *cup water*
- ☐ 1 tbsp sugar
- ☐ *salt to taste*
- ☐ 6 tbsp oil
- ☐ 25 dried chillies - *soak beforehand*
- ☐ 1 piece dried shrimp paste (blacan) *(2x2x1cm or ³/₄ x ³/₄ x ¹/₂ in)*
- ☐ 2 medium sized onions
- ☐ 1 clove garlic

} *grind to a fine paste*

Method:

Heat oil, add ground ingredients and fry till fragrant. Add sugar and salt, stir, add tamarind juice and water, then continue cooking till gravy is fairly thick. Add prawns and stir.

FRIED KANGKONG WITH BLACAN

Ingredients:

- ☐ 600g **kangkong** *(water convolvulus) - cut into 10cm (4 in) lengths and shred stalks*
- ☐ 150g shrimps - *peel*
- ☐ *salt to taste*
- ☐ 4 tbsp oil
- ☐ 1 piece dried shrimp paste (blacan) *- (2x2x1 cm or ³/₄ x ³/₄ x ¹/₂ in)*
- ☐ 2 cloves garlic
- ☐ 8 dried chillies - *soak beforehand*
- ☐ 8 shallots - *peel*

} *grind to a fine paste*

Method:

Heat oil, add ground ingredients and salt. Fry till fragrant then add shrimps. Stir, add *kangkong* stalks, stir, then add leaves. Keep stirring till vegetables are cooked. Do not overcook.

AYAM PANGGANG GAHRU

Ingredients:

- ☐ 1 chicken, weighing approximately 1.5kg - clean chicken, use whole or cut into 4 pieces
- ☐ 450g grated coconut - add 2 cups water and extract 2 cups milk
- ☐ 4 tbsp grated coconut (to be taken from the 450g) - roast over low heat till golden brown, then pound or grind into a smooth paste
- ☐ 1 fragrant lime leaf (daun limau purut)
- ☐ 2 tbsp coriander (ketumbar) powder
- ☐ 1 tsp cumin (jintan puteh) powder
- ☐ 1 stalk lemon grass (serai) - bruise
- ☐ 2 small limes (limau kesturi) - extract juice
- ☐ 6 tbsp cooking oil

Grind to a fine paste:
- ☐ 6 fresh chillies - seed for mild flavour
- ☐ 12 dried chillies - seed for mild flavour and soak to soften
- ☐ 4 candlenuts (buah keras)
- ☐ 5 shallots
- ☐ 1 small almond-sized piece of ginger

Method:

Rub roasted, ground coconut into the chicken evenly, then rub coriander and cumin powder, ground ingredients and salt. Add lime leaf and *serai*.

Heat oil in a deep pot, put in the whole chicken with all the spices and fry till fragrant. Add coconut milk and simmer. When gravy is fairly thick, remove chicken from heat, put in a tray and grill for 15-20 minutes. Remove from grill and sprinkle chicken with lime juice.

IKAN PANGGANG
(Grilled Fish)

Ingredients:

- ☐ Any medium to large sized fish may be used - e.g. Ikan Kembong, Ikan Terubok, Ikan Parang, Ikan Selar Kuning (mullet, bream, snapper etc)
- ☐ Rectangular pieces of banana leaves large enough to wrap fish

Method:

Clean the fish, make 2 diagonal cuts on each side and rub with salt. Wrap each fish in a banana leaf and grill under a gas or electric griller. Alternatively, cook over an open fire.

Serve with Sambal Asam.

SAMBAL ASAM

Ingredients:

- ☐ 1 piece dried shrimp paste (blacan) - (2x2x1 cm or $\frac{3}{4}$ x $\frac{3}{4}$ x $\frac{1}{2}$ in) - roast in dry pan
- ☐ 9 dried chillies - soak in warm water
- ☐ $\frac{1}{2}$ tbsp tamarind mixed with $\frac{1}{2}$ cup water - strain juice
- ☐ $\frac{1}{2}$ tsp salt
- ☐ 2 tsp sugar

Method:

Pound chillies and *blacan* to a fine paste, then mix with tamarind juice. Add salt and sugar and stir well.

This sauce may also be served with boiled vegetables - e.g. long beans, cabbage, *kangkong* (water convolvulus) or ladies fingers (okra).

GREEN BEANS AND SWEET POTATO LEAVES IN COCONUT MILK

Ingredients:

- ☐ 2 bundles young sweet potato leaves
- ☐ 60g dried green beans - soak overnight
- ☐ 2 red chillies
- ☐ 4 shallots
- ☐ 2 heaped tbsp small dried silverfish (ikan bilis) - soak in water for a few minutes
- ☐ 230g grated coconut - add 3 cups water and extract equal amount of milk
- ☐ salt to taste

Method:

Boil sweet potato leaves in water to which a little salt has been added. When leaves are tender, cool then cut into 6cm ($2\frac{1}{2}$in) lengths.

Boil dried green beans in water sufficient to cover them till they are cooked. Do not discard water. Pound or grind chillies and shallots to a fine paste then add *ikan bilis* and pound coarsely.

In a deep pot, put the chopped leaves, cooked green beans and the little cooking water that is left, ground ingredients, coconut milk and salt. Bring to the boil and cook over low heat for another 10 minutes, stirring frequently.

Serve with a side dish of unripe mango to which salt and birds-eye chilli (*chilli padi*) have been added.

Note: When buying dried green beans, choose the big variety.

Green Beans and
Sweet Potato Leaves in
Coconut Milk

Nangka Lemak

Ikan Panggang

Sambal Asam

NANGKA LEMAK
(Jack Fruit in Coconut Milk)

Ingredients:

- [ ] **450g young unripe jackfruit (nangka)** - *peel and cut into slices about 3cm (1¹/₄ in) thick (oil knife before cutting)*
- [ ] **450g grated coconut** - *first add 2 cups water and extract equal amount of milk (thick milk): add another 2 cups of water and extract equal amount of milk (thin milk)*
- [ ] **120g salted ikan kurau bones, or dried salted cod** - *wash*
- [ ] **150g shrimps** - *peel and de-vein*
- [ ] **4 sprigs basil (daun selaseh), optional** - *break each into 3 pieces*
- [ ] **salt to taste**
- [ ] **2 tsp small white dried silver fish (ikan bilis)** - *soak beforehand*
- [ ] **5 shallots**
- [ ] **¹/₂ tsp black peppercorns**
- [ ] **2 dried chillies** - *soak to soften*
- [ ] **1 thin slice fresh turmeric*

} *grind coarsely*

Method:

Boil *nangka* in salted water for about 10 minutes or until half cooked. Drain and put in a large pot with salt fish bones, shrimps, salt, *daun selaseh*, ground ingredients and thin coconut milk.

Bring to the boil over medium heat, stirring while it is cooking. Boil for a minute or two then add thick coconut milk. Bring back to the boil over low heat, and cook stirring all the time for 10-15 minutes.

Note: 450g of *nangka* is approximately one quarter of a small fruit.

MIXED VEGETABLES
(Malay Style)

Ingredients:

- [ ] **3 tbsp oil**
- [ ] **1 tbsp sesame oil**
- [ ] **2 big onions** - *cut into wedges*
- [ ] **2 cloves garlic** - *chop*
- [ ] **2 red chillies** - *slice diagonally*
- [ ] **200g cauliflower** - *cut into florets*
- [ ] **1 medium carrot** - *slice diagonally (not too thin)*
- [ ] **5g black fungus** - *soak 10 mins*
- [ ] **salt to taste**
- [ ] **2 medium sized sotong** - *clean, cut body in half then into pieces - slash edges of each piece*
- [ ] **1 green capsicum** - *cut into half, then slice*
- [ ] **10 pcs minicorn** - *cut in half*
- [ ] **200g medium prawns** - *peel, remove head, de-vein*
- [ ] **100g snow peas** - *cut in 2 if too large*
- [ ] **1 tbsp light soya sauce**
- [ ] **4 stalks spring greens (chye sim)** - *separate stalks from leaves - cut or break into 4cm lengths*
- [ ] **4 red chillies split in two lengthwise**
- [ ] **pepper**
- [ ] **¹/₂ cup water**
- [ ] **2 tbsp cornflour**
- [ ] **¹/₄ cup water**

} *combine*

Method:

Heat oil, (2 kinds) add onion wedges, stir. Add garlic, sliced chilli, carrot, cauliflower, black fungus and salt. Sprinkle some water from allowance and stir well.
Add sotong, stir then add capsicum and minicorn. Stir then add prawns and snow peas. Sprinkle with more water. Stir and leave to cook for a few minutes. Add a dash of pepper and soya sauce. Add spring green stalks first then leaves. Add chilli halves and salt to taste. Finally add cornflour mixture and mix well.

Vegetables should not be overcooked.

Note: With stir fry dishes, always stir and mix ingredients after each addition.

MALAY CHICKEN RICE

Ingredients:

- [ ] 1 chicken (approx. 1.25kg)
- [ ] 2-3 fragrant screwpine leaves (daun pandan) - *tie into knot*
- [ ] 1 piece ginger (size of walnut) - *bruise*
- [ ] 1 tsp salt
- [ ] sufficient water to cover chicken

For rubbing on cooked chicken:

- [ ] 2 cloves garlic
- [ ] 1 pc ginger (size of walnut) } *grind fine*
- [ ] Add 1 tsp turmeric powder (kunyit) *to above paste*
- [ ] salt to taste
- [ ] 1½ tsp honey
- [ ] lettuce leaves
- [ ] slices of cucumber and tomato } *for garnishing*
- [ ] fried shallot

Method for cooking chicken:

Put water, salt, screwpine leaves and ginger in a deep pot and bring to the boil. When boiling, add chicken and boil for ten minutes. Remove chicken and put on dish.

Keep stock aside for cooking rice and for soup.

Rub ginger-garlic paste and salt over chicken while still hot.

Next, rub honey over it.

Heat oil for deep frying in wok. Add chicken and reduce heat to medium. Fry till brown.

Ingredients for rice:

- [ ] 500g rice - *wash and drain*
- [ ] 2 shallots
- [ ] 2 cloves garlic } *chop fine*
- [ ] 1½ tbsp sesame oil
- [ ] 2 fragrant screwpine leaves (daun pandan) - *tie into knot*

Method:

Heat oil, add chopped shallots and garlic. When fragrant, add rice. Fry for 5 minutes, coating the rice grains with oil. Put rice into pot, add 2½ cups chicken stock and cook.

Ingredients for soup:

- [ ] chicken stock
- [ ] chicken feet and gizzard
- [ ] 1 stalk Chinese celery
- [ ] 2 stalks spring onion } *chop*
- [ ] salt to taste
- [ ] pepper
- [ ] fried shallots - *for garnishing*

Method:

Re-boil left over chicken stock with chicken feet and gizzard. When boiling, add celery and spring onion. Add seasoning. Before serving, remove chicken feet and gizzard and garnish with chopped shallots.

Ingredients for chilli sauce:

- [ ] 15 dried chillies - *soak*
- [ ] 10 red chillies
- [ ] 2 cloves garlic
- [ ] ½ cup water
  Put all the above ingredients in liquidiser and grind fine.
- [ ] ½ cup water
- [ ] 2 tbsp brown sugar
- [ ] salt to taste
- [ ] juice of 3 limes

Method:

Put ground ingredients in saucepan, add water, brown sugar and salt. Cook till thick. Remove from heat and add lime juice.

To serve:

Chop chicken into pieces. Arrange on a bed of lettuce. Garnish with cucumber and tomato slices.

Sprinkle fried shallot over rice. Serve individual bowls of soup.

STEAMED CHILLI FISH

Mixed Vegetables (Malay style)

Ingredients:

- [ ] *1 white pomfret (approx. 600g in weight) - make 2 slashes on each side of fish, rub with salt and wash well*
- [ ] *6 - 8 lettuce leaves*
- [ ] *5 tbsp oil*
- [ ] *Juice of 3 limes (cut up skin of lime into little pieces for garnishing)*

For sauce:

- [ ] *12 red chillies*
- [ ] *2 cloves garlic*
- [ ] *3 stalks lemon grass (serai) - root end*
- [ ] *1 big onion*
- [ ] *1 pc galangal (lengkuas) - size of walnut*
- [ ] *1 cm pc fresh turmeric*
- [ ] *$^1/_2$ cup water*

Method:

Chop all above ingredients for sauce into small pieces. Put in liquidiser and grind. The consistency should be thick. Heat oil, add ground ingredients and salt to taste. Fry till fragrant. Add lime juice and stir.

Boil water in steamer. Steam fish for 20 minutes.

To serve:

Arrange lettuce leaves on a platter, pour some of the sauce on leaves, put fish over sauce and pour the rest of the sauce over fish.

Garnish with lime skin.

Steamed Chilli Fish

Malay Chicken Rice

Chicken Soup

Chilli Sauce

59

Sambal Empat Sekawan

Tahu Belado

Taukwa with Vegetable and Chicken Filling

Steamed Tahu with Minced Chicken

Tahu Telor with Peanut Sauce

STEAMED TAHU WITH MINCED CHICKEN

Ingredients:

- ☐ **500g tahu** - *split horizontally into two*
- ☐ **10 straw mushrooms** - *slice fine*
- ☐ **200g boneless chicken breast** - *mince or chop fine*
- ☐ **2 stalks spring onion** ⎫
- ☐ **2 stalks Chinese celery** ⎬ *chop fine*
- ☐ **2 red chillies** - *remove seeds and chop fine*
- ☐ **3 tbsp light soya sauce**
- ☐ **1 tsp ground white pepper**
- ☐ **2 tsp cornflour**

Method:

Boil water in steamer.

Put tahu halves on a plate for steaming. Prick tahu.

Combine the rest of the ingredients in a bowl. Divide mixture in two and put over each half of tahu.

Steam tahu for 15-20 minutes.

TAHU BELADO

Ingredients:

- ☐ **3-4 hard beancurd (taukwa)** - *cut in 2 diagonally and deep fry till lightly brown*

- ☐ **3 tbsp oil**
- ☐ **2 medium sized onions** ⎫
- ☐ **5 red chillies** ⎬ *grind coarsely*
- ☐ **1 garlic** ⎭
- ☐ **salt to taste**
- ☐ **juice of 3 limes**

Method:

Heat oil, add ground ingredients and salt. Fry till fragrant. Add lime juice, stir, add beancurd. Stir and mix well.

SAMBAL EMPAT SEKAWAN

(Sambal Taukwa, Eggs, Ikan Bilis and Prawns)

Ingredients:

- [ ] *2 pieces hard beancurd* (taukwa) - *cut each into 9 pieces*
- [ ] *50g dried anchovies* (ikan bilis) - *split in two, rinse, drain and dry*
- [ ] *300g prawns or shrimps - remove head and shell and de-vein*
- [ ] *5 - 6 hard boiled eggs - make slashes on surface of each*
- [ ] *oil for frying*
- [ ] *3 tbsp palm sugar* (gula Melaka)
- [ ] *$^1/_2$ tbsp tamarind pulp - mix with $^1/_2$ cup water and strain for juice*
- [ ] *3 onions - cut in half then into thick slices*
- [ ] *salt to taste*
- [ ] *4 tbsp oil*

Put in a blender with a little water and grind fine:-
- [ ] *1 large onion*
- [ ] *30 dried chillies - soak beforehand*
- [ ] *1 clove garlic*

Method:

Shallow fry first, the beancurd, then ikan bilis separately till lightly brown. Remove from heat and keep aside.

Shallow fry prawns till they turn pink. Keep aside.

Heat 4 tbsp oil. Add ground ingredients, salt, sugar and tamarind juice. Bring to the boil. When mixture is fragrant and thick, add fried beancurd, ikan bilis, prawns and eggs. Stir well for 5 minutes. Add onions. When onions are cooked, remove from heat.

TAHU TELOR WITH PEANUT SAUCE

Ingredients:

- [ ] *3 pieces hard beancurd* (taukwa) - *mash with a fork*
- [ ] *5 eggs - add a little salt and beat*
- [ ] *200g beansprouts - remove tails and scald*
- [ ] *6 - 8 lettuce leaves - wash and shred coarsely*
- [ ] *1 cucumber - cut in strips*
- [ ] *2 tbsp oil*
- [ ] *6 red chillies*
- [ ] *8 chilli padi (optional) - for a hotter sauce*   } *For sauce: Combine in blender and grind till fine*
- [ ] *1 clove garlic*
- [ ] *$^1/_4$ cup water*
- [ ] *1 cup water*
- [ ] *2 tbsp brown sugar* or *4 tbsp palm sugar* (gula Melaka)
- [ ] *salt to taste*
- [ ] *1 cup peanuts - roast till brown, cool then remove skin and grind coarsely*
- [ ] *Juice of 3 limes - cut up lime skin for use as well* or *1 tbsp vinegar*
- [ ] *1 tbsp dark soya sauce*

Method for sauce:

Put blended ingredients in saucepan, add water, sugar and salt and bring to the boil. Add ground peanut, stir and bring back to the boil. When thick, add soya sauce, lime juice and lime skin. Stir and remove from heat.

Method for Tahu Telor:

Heat oil in omelette pan. Pour in one large ladleful of egg, put half the mashed beancurd over it and add more egg to cover. When set, turn omelette over.

Makes two large omelettes.

To serve:

Put omelette on plate, sprinkle bean sprouts and cucumber over it. Pour sauce over and garnish with shredded lettuce.

TAUKWA WITH VEGETABLE AND CHICKEN FILLING

Ingredients:

- [ ] 2 tbsp oil
- [ ] 4 shallots
- [ ] 1 clove garlic
- [ ] 1 red chilli
- [ ] 4 chilli padi (optional)

} chop

- [ ] 1 small chicken thigh or breast - debone and chop meat into small pieces
- [ ] 1 small carrot - peel and shred or cut into fine strips
- [ ] 2 tbsp light soya sauce
- [ ] 100g cabbage - shred or cut fine
- [ ] 2 tbsp water
- [ ] $^1/_2$ bundle bean thread vermicelli (sohoon) - soak and cut into short lengths
- [ ] 5 pieces hard beancurd (taukwa) - cut in half diagonally
- [ ] 10 small lettuce leaves and 10 chilli padi - for garnishing

Method:

Heat oil, add chopped ingredients. When fragrant, add chicken then carrot and soya sauce, stirring after each addition. Add cabbage and water. Stir and leave to cook for a couple of minutes. Add sohoon. Mix well. When vegetables are cooked but not too soft, remove from heat.

Deep fry bean curd halves till lightly brown. When a little cool, slit taukwa along the long side and spoon cooked filling into each.

Garnish each piece with a small lettuce leaf and chilli padi.

NORTH INDIAN CHICKEN CURRY

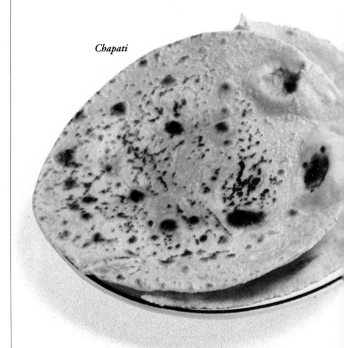

Chapati

Ingredients:

- [ ] *1 chicken weighing about 1.75kg - cut into fairly large pieces and remove skin*
- [ ] *1 tsp turmeric powder*
- [ ] *2 tbsp plain yoghurt*
- [ ] *1³/₄ cups water*
- [ ] *salt to taste*
- [ ] *3 onions - grate*
- [ ] *8 tbsp oil*

Roast in dry pan till lightly brown:

- [ ] *4 level tbsp coriander (ketumbar) seeds*
- [ ] *1 tsp cumin (jintan puteh) seeds*
- [ ] *18 dried chillies - break each into 3 pieces*

Method:

Grind roasted ingredients. In a bowl, combine chicken with ground spices, turmeric powder, salt, yoghurt and ¹/₄ cup water from allowance.

Heat oil, add chicken, fry till fragrant, then add onion.

Stir fry for a while then add 1¹/₂ cups water, cover and cook over low heat.

When chicken is tender and gravy a little thick, remove from heat.

Watery Dhal

North Indian Chicken Curry

Kheema

Alu

Gajjar Chutney

WATERY DHAL

Ingredients:

- [ ] 1 cup yellow lentils (dhal) - soak for about 3 hours, then wash, remove skin and drain
- [ ] 3 cups water
- [ ] 1/2 onion - slice thick
- [ ] 2 green chillies - slit lengthwise
- [ ] 2 cloves garlic - cut into thick slices
- [ ] 1 stick cinnamon - 3cm (1 1/4 in) long
- [ ] 3 cloves
- [ ] 1 1/2 tsp turmeric powder
- [ ] salt to taste

Method:

Combine all the ingredients in a deep pot; stir to mix, then boil till dhal is soft; remove from heat.

Ingredients for frying:

- [ ] 1/2 onion - slice finely
- [ ] 1 tsp cumin (jintan puteh) seeds - grind coarsely
- [ ] 3 dried chillies - break each into 3 pieces
- [ ] 2 tbsp ghee

Method:

Heat ghee, then fry the above ingredients till fragrant and onions brown; pour ghee and fried ingredients immediately into cooked dhal, cover the pot for a minute then serve.

ALU
(Potato Curry)

Ingredients:

- [ ] 600g potatoes - scrub well, boil and cut each into 6 wedges; do not peel
- [ ] 1 tsp coriander (ketumbar) seeds } roast in dry pan
- [ ] 6 dried chillies } and grind coarsely
- [ ] 1/2 tsp turmeric powder
- [ ] 1 large tomato - chop coarsely
- [ ] 1 medium sized onion - grate coarsely
- [ ] 1 cup water
- [ ] salt to taste
- [ ] 6 tbsp oil

Method:

Heat oil, add potatoes and stir fry. Add ground ingredients and turmeric powder, stir, add onion, tomato and water, stir, add salt and leave to cook till gravy is quite thick.

KHEEMA
(Minced Meat Curry)

Ingredients:

- [ ] 230g minced beef or mutton
- [ ] 4 slices ginger (each 1cm thick) } grind to a
- [ ] 3 cloves garlic } fine paste
- [ ] 3 tbsp meat curry powder
- [ ] 2 cups water
- [ ] salt to taste
- [ ] 1 small bunch coriander leaves - chop
- [ ] 120g green peas
- [ ] 1 green chilli - slice thinly
- [ ] 2 medium sized potatoes - peel } cut into
- [ ] 2 medium sized tomatoes } small cubes
- [ ] 1 big onion }
- [ ] 1/2 onion - slice thinly }
- [ ] 3 cardamoms } ingredients
- [ ] 4 cloves } for frying
- [ ] 1 stick cinnamon - 4cm (1 1/2 in) long }
- [ ] 6 tbsp oil

Method:

In a bowl, combine minced meat with ginger-garlic paste, curry powder, salt and 1/2 cup water from allowance.

Heat oil, add ingredients for frying. When onions are brown, add minced meat and fry till fragrant. Add potatoes, stir, then add 1 1/2 cups water and bring to the boil. Cover and continue cooking till potatoes are soft, stirring now and then. Add tomatoes, onion, peas and chilli, cover and cook for 3-5 minutes.

When serving, sprinkle with chopped coriander leaves.

CRISPY MUTTON CHOPS

Ingredients:

- [ ] 6 lamb or mutton chops
- [ ] white of 3 eggs
- [ ] 1 tbsp honey
- [ ] 1 tbsp dark soya sauce
- [ ] 1 1/2 tbsp fine bread crumbs
- [ ] oil for deep frying

Method:

Boil mutton with 1 tsp salt and 1 tsp pepper for 30 minutes in just enough water to cover.

Combine egg white with honey, soya sauce and bread crumbs. Dip the boiled chops into mixture and deep fry.

Serve with lemon wedges or mint sauce, potato chips and green peas.

CHAPATI

Ingredients:
- [ ] 450g fine wholemeal flour (atta)
- [ ] 2 tbsp cooking oil
- [ ] 1 cup water mixed with 1 tsp salt

Method:

Sieve flour into a bowl. Make a hollow in the centre and pour oil into it. Rub oil into flour then add half the amount of water. Knead well for 10 minutes to form a soft dough.

Add the rest of the water gradually. Knead for another 10 minutes then cover with damp cloth and leave to stand for 45 minutes to 1 hour. Divide dough into balls the size of walnuts, and roll each on lightly floured board into thin, round pancakes.

Heat griddle (tawa) or a heavy-based frying pan. When very hot, put one chapati on it. When small blisters appear on the surface, cook other side. Leave for a second then press lightly with a folded tea towel so that bubbles appear and when lightly brown, remove and wrap in a tea towel till ready to serve.

Brush a little ghee or oil on one side before serving.(Optional)

Note: Leaving the dough to stand before rolling, and pressing chapatis with a tea towel while cooking make the chapatis light.

GAJJAR CHUTNEY
(Carrot Chutney)

Ingredients:
- [ ] 150g carrot - cut into thick strips
- [ ] 2 tbsp tomato puree
- [ ] 2 tbsp vinegar   } combine
- [ ] 1 tbsp sugar
- [ ] $^1/_2$ tsp salt
- [ ] 2 tbsp oil
- [ ] 2 cloves garlic - grind fine
- [ ] $^1/_2$ tsp mustard seeds
- [ ] $^1/_2$ tsp chilli powder
- [ ] $^1/_4$ tsp cumin powder

Method:

Heat oil, add garlic and mustard seeds. When brown, add tomato puree mixture. Boil and remove from heat. Add spice powders. Stir, pour over carrot and mix well

Note: Serve with meat dishes. May be stored in a jar.

SAVOURY RICE WITH CURRIED LAMB

Ingredients for Curried Lamb:
- [ ] 450g lamb - cut into small squares
- [ ] 2 tbsp meat curry powder
- [ ] 2 tsp tomato paste
- [ ] 1 tsp peppercorns - grind coarsely
- [ ] 1 large onion   } cut into small squares
- [ ] 2 tomatoes
- [ ] 1 tbsp plain yoghurt
- [ ] salt to taste
- [ ] 1 slice ginger - 1cm ($^1/_2$ in) thick
- [ ] 2 cloves garlic   } grind to a fine paste
- [ ] 1 red chilli
- [ ] 1 green chilli

Combine lamb with all the above ingredients and marinate for a while.

- [ ] 2 tbsp ghee
- [ ] $^1/_2$ onion - slice thinly
- [ ] 2 cups water
- [ ] 4 potatoes - peel and cut into 6 pieces lengthwise
- [ ] 20 - 30 cashew nuts - fry in oil till golden brown
- [ ] 1 small bunch big coriander leaves   } For garnishing
- [ ] 1 small bunch mint leaves

Method:

Heat ghee in pot and fry sliced onion till golden brown; add marinated meat and stir-fry for 1 or 2 minutes until fragrant. Add water, bring to the boil then add potatoes. Cover pot and simmer till meat is tender and the gravy fairly thick.

Ingredients for rice:
- [ ] 600g Basmati rice - wash and drain
- [ ] 1.6 litres (6$^1/_2$ cups) water
- [ ] 1 tsp salt
- [ ] 1 tbsp ghee

For garnishing:
- [ ] 4 tbsp raisins   } fry in ghee
- [ ] sliced almonds

Method:

Bring water to the boil, add salt and rice and boil for 10-15 minutes checking often to see if rice is cooked. When rice is cooked, drain, then rinse rice in the strainer by pouring more boiling water over it to remove any excess starch. Mix ghee with rice. Make a ring with rice in an ovenproof dish. Put curried lamb in hollow of ring and bake in a moderate oven for 10 minutes. Garnish rice with raisins and almonds, and curry with cashew nuts, coriander and mint leaves.

STUFFED CHICKEN LEGS

Ingredients:
- [ ] *2 chicken drumsticks and 2 thighs (approx. 450g)*
  - *make a slit about 5cm (2 in) long near the bone of each piece; rub chicken with salt and pepper*
- [ ] *oil for deep frying*

For Stuffing:
- [ ] *4-5 small florets of cauliflower* } *chop fine*
- [ ] *1 small carrot*
- [ ] *5 French beans - slice very thin*
- [ ] *1 tsp coriander (ketumbar) powder*
- [ ] *$\frac{1}{2}$ tsp chilli powder*
- [ ] *$\frac{1}{2}$ tsp turmeric powder*
- [ ] *$2\frac{1}{2}$ tbsp water*
- [ ] *a few mint leaves - chop fine*
- [ ] *salt to taste*
- [ ] *$1\frac{1}{2}$ tbsp oil*

Method:
Heat oil, add vegetables and stir fry. After a minute or two, add coriander, chilli and turmeric powder, mint leaves and salt. Fry, then add water and cook till vegetables are soft and dry. Leave to cool.

To stuff chicken:
Spoon stuffing into cavity of chicken legs and secure with thread.

To cook:
Heat oil then deep fry chicken over lot heat.

Note: For this dish, use chicken thighs and drumsticks only. Prepare the stuffing first, giving it time to cool.

EGG AND LAMB (OR BEEF) KEBAB

Ingredients:
- [ ] *230g minced lamb or beef*
- [ ] *3-4 sprigs big coriander leaves - chop fine*
- [ ] *1 tsp pepper*
- [ ] *1 tsp chilli powder*
- [ ] *1 tsp coriander (ketumbar) powder*
- [ ] *$\frac{1}{4}$ tsp turmeric powder*
- [ ] *1 slice toast - crush into fine crumbs*
- [ ] *2 egg yolks*
- [ ] *2 green chillies - chop into small pieces*
- [ ] *1 chopped onion (optional)*
- [ ] *5 hard boiled eggs*
- [ ] *oil for deep frying*

Method:
Combine all ingredients (except hard boiled eggs) in a bowl and mix well.

Divide mixture into five portions. Wrap one portion around each egg, then deep fry till golden brown. Cut eggs in half, serve on a bed of lettuce with raw onion rings, and mint or chilli sauce.

Crispy Mutton Chops

Egyptian Salata

Savoury Rice with Curried Lamb

Egg and Lamb Kebab

Minced Chicken Kebab

Stuffed Chicken Legs

69

EGYPTIAN SALATA

Ingredients:

- [ ] 100g cauliflower - *cut into small florets*
- [ ] 1 small carrot - *cut into strips or cubes*
- [ ] 8 french beans - *cut into small pieces*
- [ ] ¹/₂ medium size cucumber - *remove seeds and cut into small cubes*
- [ ] 2 tomatoes - *remove seeds and cut into small cubes*
- [ ] 2 green chillies
- [ ] juice of ¹/₂ lemon
- [ ] 4 sprigs coriander leaves ⎫
- [ ] 4 sprigs mint leaves ⎭ *chop*
- [ ] 4 tbsp vinegar
- [ ] 1 tbsp sugar
- [ ] pinch of salt
- [ ] ¹/₂ tsp black pepper
- [ ] ¹/₂ tsp chilli powder
- [ ] ¹/₂ tsp cumin powder

Method:

Dissolve sugar and salt in vinegar. Add spice powders, stir and cool. Combine all vegetables in a bowl, pour lemon juice over then pour cooled vinegar. Mix well. Sprinkle coriander and mint leaves over vegetables.

MINCED CHICKEN KEBAB

Ingredients:

- [ ] 230g chicken meat - *mince*
- [ ] 1 small bunch coriander leaves ⎫
- [ ] 1 small bunch mint leaves ⎭ *chop fine*
- [ ] 1 tbsp coriander (ketumbar) *powder*
- [ ] 1 tsp chilli powder
- [ ] ¹/₂ tsp turmeric powder
- [ ] 1 tsp black pepper
- [ ] 1¹/₂ tbsp golden bread crumbs
- [ ] salt to taste
- [ ] oil for deep frying

Method:

Combine all ingredients except oil in a bowl. Mix well and shape into small ovals. Deep fry till golden brown.
Serve with chilli or mint sauce.

COCONUT SAMBAL

Ingredients:

- [ ] 1 cup grated coconut
- [ ] 5 shallots - *peel*
- [ ] 2 green chillies
- [ ] 1¹/₂ tsp tamarind - *remove seed*
- [ ] 1cm (¹/₂ in) cube ginger
- [ ] 1 clove garlic
- [ ] 1 sprig curry leaves (**karuvapillai**) - *discard stalk*
- [ ] ¹/₂ tsp salt

Method:

Grind coconut, then add chillies, ginger, garlic, salt, tamarind and shallots. When these have been ground to a fine paste, put into a serving dish.

Note: This sambal tastes best when traditional grinding stone is used to grind ingredients.

Mutton Chops with gravy

Egg Curry with Shrimps and Potatoes

Dried Mutton Chops

Coconut Sambal

Kitchree Rice

71

MUTTON CHOPS WITH GRAVY

Ingredients:

- [ ] 600g mutton or lamb chops *(about 8 chops)*
- [ ] 6 green chillies
- [ ] 4 red chillies ⎫
- [ ] 3 slices ginger *(each 1cm or ½ in thick)* ⎬ *grind to a fine paste*
- [ ] 5 cloves garlic ⎭
- [ ] 2 tbsp plain yoghurt or juice of 1 lime
- [ ] 2 tbsp coriander (ketumbar) *powder*
- [ ] 1 tbsp chilli powder
- [ ] 2 onions - *chop*
- [ ] 4 tomatoes - *chop*
- [ ] 6 stalks coriander leaves - *chop*
- [ ] salt to taste
- [ ] 1 small onion - *slice thinly* ⎫
- [ ] 4 cardamoms ⎬ *ingredients for frying*
- [ ] 5 cloves
- [ ] 1 stick cinnamon 5cm (2 in) long ⎭
- [ ] 10 tbsp oil
- [ ] 4 cups water

Method:

In a large bowl, combine chops with all the ingredients except ingredients for frying, oil and water. Heat oil, add ingredients for frying. When fragrant, add mutton and fry till fragrant then add water. Cover and boil, removing cover and stirring from time to time. Continue cooking till mutton is tender and the gravy is very thick.

DRIED MUTTON CHOPS

Ingredients:

- [ ] 450g mutton or lamb chops *(about 6 pieces)*
- [ ] 1 tbsp chilli powder
- [ ] 1 tsp turmeric powder
- [ ] 1 tbsp coriander (ketumbar) *powder*
- [ ] ½ tsp black pepper powder
- [ ] salt to taste
- [ ] 1 tsp cumin (jintan puteh) *seeds - soak then crush coarsely*
- [ ] ¼ cup water
- [ ] 6 tbsp oil
- [ ] 1 cup water
- [ ] 1 small bunch small coriander leaves *for garnishing*

Method:

Mix all the spices, salt and ¼ cup water into a paste, and then rub paste over chops.

Heat oil, add chops and fry till fragrant. Add water, cover pan and cook over low heat. When meat is tender and moisture absorbed, remove from heat and drain. Garnish with small coriander leaves and serve hot.

EGG CURRY WITH SHRIMPS AND POTATOES

Ingredients:

- [ ] 5 eggs - *boil and shell, then make long, shallow cuts on the surface of each egg*
- [ ] 300g shrimps - *peel and de-vein*

Combine in a bowl:

- [ ] 6 tbsp fish curry powder
- [ ] 1 tbsp grated coconut - *grind fine*
- [ ] ½ onion - *slice thickly*
- [ ] 3 cloves garlic - *slice thickly*
- [ ] 1 green chilli ⎫
- [ ] 1 red chilli ⎬ *slash*
- [ ] 1 sprig curry leaves (karuvapillai)
- [ ] 1½ tbsp tamarind - *add 3 cups water and strain juice*

- [ ] 1 tsp fish curry spices ⎫
- [ ] 1 sprig curry leaves (karuvapillai) ⎬ *ingredients for frying*
- [ ] ½ onion - *thinly sliced* ⎭
- [ ] 6 small potatoes - *halve and leave unpeeled*
- [ ] 4 tbsp oil

Method:

Heat oil, add potatoes and ingredients for frying. Fry till potatoes and onions are brown, then add ingredients combined in a bowl. Cover and bring to the boil. When potatoes are almost cooked, add eggs and shrimps. Continue boiling till potatoes are cooked.

VEGETARIAN KHEEMA

Ingredients:

- [ ] **300g carrot** - cut into sections and each section into quarters or 6 pieces
- [ ] **250g cauliflower** - cut into small florets
- [ ] **2 medium onions** ⎫
- [ ] **2 cloves garlic** ⎬ grind fine in liquidiser
- [ ] **2 medium tomatoes** ⎪
- [ ] **2 sprigs coriander leaves** ⎭
- [ ] **2 tbsp coriander powder (ketumbar)** ⎫
- [ ] **$^1/_2$ tbsp chilli powder** ⎬ add to ground mixture
- [ ] **1 tsp turmeric powder (kunyit)** ⎪
- [ ] **$^1/_2$ tsp cumin powder (jintan puteh)** ⎭
- [ ] **6 cloves**
- [ ] **4 cardamoms**
- [ ] **4cm length cinnamon stick**
- [ ] **5 tbsp oil**
- [ ] **salt**
- [ ] **2 tbsp tomato puree**
- [ ] **1 cup water**
- [ ] **1 $^1/_2$ cups green peas**
- [ ] **2 tomatoes** - chop
- [ ] **4 sprigs coriander leaves** - chop

Method:

Half cook carrots, then cauliflower in boiling salted water. Strain and keep aside.

Heat oil, add ground ingredients, whole spices and salt to taste. Fry till fragrant. Add tomato puree and cook over low heat till oil rises to surface. Add water and carrot, increase heat, cover and cook for 10 mins. Add cauliflower, cover and cook for 5 mins. Add green peas. When vegetables are soft, add tomato and cook for a minute. Add coriander leaves just before serving.

Serve with rice, chapati or naan.

KITCHREE RICE

Ingredients:

- [ ] **600g Basmati rice** - wash and drain
- [ ] **170g yellow lentils (dhal)** - soak for 2 hours, wash and drain
- [ ] **1 medium size onion** - slice thin
- [ ] **1 stick cinnamon 5cm (2 in) long** ⎫
- [ ] **2 cardamoms** ⎬ ingredients for frying
- [ ] **4 cloves** ⎪
- [ ] **2 fragrant screwpine leaves (daun pandan)** - wash and tie ⎭
- [ ] **5 small cloves garlic** ⎫
- [ ] **1 slice ginger (1cm or $^1/_2$ in thick)** ⎬ grind to a smooth paste
- [ ] **3 slightly heaped tbsp ghee**
- [ ] **water** - equal in volume to amount of rice used
- [ ] **1 tbsp plain yoghurt**
- [ ] **1 small tin evaporated milk (170g)**
- [ ] **$^1/_2$ tsp yellow food colouring**
- [ ] **salt to taste**

Method:

Combine rice with dhal in a bowl.

Heat ghee, fry onion, cinnamon, cardamom, cloves, pandan leaves and ginger-garlic paste till fragrant.

Add water, yoghurt, milk, salt and colouring. Bring to the boil. As soon as it boils, add rice and dhal, stir, cover and leave to cook. Lower heat when amount of water is reduced. Continue cooking till water is absorbed, then stir rice and continue cooking over very low heat, keeping pot covered.

When steam emits from pot, rice is cooked. If preferred, colouring may be added when rice is almost cooked.

Green Bean Dhal

Vegetarian Korma

Okra Kheema

OKRA KHEEMA

Ingredients:

- [ ] 300g okra (ladies fingers) - *slice thin*
- [ ] 2 onions
- [ ] 2 cloves garlic
- [ ] 2 green chillies } *chop fine*
- [ ] 5 tbsp oil
- [ ] 1 tsp turmeric powder (kunyit)
- [ ] 2 tsp chilli powder
- [ ] 1 tsp coriander powder (ketumbar)
- [ ] $^1/_2$ tsp cumin powder (jintan puteh)
- [ ] juice of 1 lime
- [ ] salt to taste
- [ ] 2 large tomatoes - *chop*

Method:

Heat oil, add chopped ingredients. Fry till onions are soft and slightly brown. Add okra, mix well. Add spice powders, salt and lime juice and mix well. Add tomato, stir and cook till soft.

Serve with chapati or plain boiled rice.

Vegetarian Kheema

VEGETARIAN KORMA

Ingredients:

- [ ] 300g small potatoes (*use new potatoes if available*)
- [ ] 1 carrot (approx. 200g) - *cut into sections and each section into 4 or 6 pcs.*
- [ ] 200g cauliflower - *cut into florets*
- [ ] 100g minicorn - *cut each in half*
- [ ] 100g french beans - *cut into 4cm lengths*
- [ ] 2 onions
- [ ] 4 medium tomatoes
- [ ] 4 sprigs mint leaves } *grind fine in liquidiser*
- [ ] 3 green chillies
- [ ] 2 cloves garlic
- [ ] 2 tbsp coriander powder (ketumbar)
- [ ] 1 tsp turmeric powder (kunyit) } *add to ground mixture*
- [ ] $^1/_2$ tsp cumin powder (jintan puteh)
- [ ] $^1/_2$ tsp black pepper
- [ ] 6 cloves
- [ ] 4-5 cardamoms
- [ ] 2 pcs (4cm length) cinnamon stick
- [ ] 1 cup water
- [ ] salt
- [ ] 30 cashew nuts - *roast or fry till brown*
- [ ] 10 cherry tomatoes
    or 3 tomatoes - cut into quarters then halve each piece
- [ ] juice of 1 lemon
- [ ] 2 sprigs coriander leaves
- [ ] 2 sprigs mint leaves } *chop*
- [ ] 6 tbsp oil

Method:

Boil separately in salted water each of the following vegetables:

potatoes, carrots, cauliflower, minicorn and beans. Strain and put aside. Only <u>half cook</u> the vegetables. Cut potatoes in half.

Heat oil, add ground ingredients and whole spices. When fragrant, add salt, potatoes and water. Stir then add carrot and cauliflower and cook for 5 minutes. Add corn and beans, mix, add lemon juice. Stir, add cashew nuts then tomatoes. Mix well. Finally, add chopped coriander and mint leaves.

Serve with rice, chapati or naan

GREEN BEAN DHAL

Ingredients:
- [ ] *1 cup green beans - clean, remove stones, wash and drain*
- [ ] *5 cups water*
- [ ] *1 tsp turmeric powder (kunyit)*
- [ ] *salt to taste*
- [ ] *5 tbsp oil*

Ingredients for frying:
- [ ] *1 clove garlic*   } *chop*
- [ ] *2cm thick piece of ginger*
- [ ] *2 tomatoes*
- [ ] *1 onion*   } *grind fine in liquidiser*
- [ ] *2 green chillies*
- [ ] *2 cloves garlic*
- [ ] *2 tsp coriander powder (ketumbar)*   } *add to ground mixture*
- [ ] *1 tsp cumin powder (jintan puteh)*
- [ ] *1 tsp chilli powder*
- [ ] *2 tomatoes*   } *chop*
- [ ] *4 sprigs coriander leaves*

Method:

Put beans in pot with water, turmeric powder and salt and boil till soft.

Heat oil, add chopped ginger-garlic. Fry till brown. Add ground ingredients and fry till fragrant. Add this to boiling beans (oil included) when beans are almost soft. Continue boiling for another 10 minutes. Add chopped tomato and coriander leaves. Boil for 2-3 mins. more.

PILAU RICE WITH CASHEW NUTS

Ingredients:
- [ ] *600g Basmati rice - wash and drain*
- [ ] *4 tbsp ghee*
- [ ] *1 stick cinnamon 4cm (1 1/2 in) long*   } *ingredients for frying*
- [ ] *4 cloves*
- [ ] *4 cardamoms*
- [ ] *1 piece ginger - size of a walnut*   } *grind to a fine paste*
- [ ] *3 cloves garlic*
- [ ] *3 tbsp plain yoghurt*
- [ ] *water - equal in volume to the amount of rice used*
- [ ] *5 tbsp evaporated milk*
- [ ] *salt to taste*
- [ ] *1 tbsp rose water*
- [ ] *120g cashew nuts - fry in ghee and put aside for garnishing*

Method:

Heat ghee, add ingredients for frying and ginger-garlic paste. Fry till fragrant, then add yoghurt, water, evaporated milk, salt and rose water and bring to the boil. When boiling, add rice and continue boiling. When rice is drying, reduce heat. Keep pot covered and cook over low heat. When fragrance emits from pot, stir to turn rice over. Cover pot and cook for another 5 minutes, then sprinkle cashew nuts over top.

MINCED MUTTON BALLS

Ingredients:
- [ ] *230g minced mutton*
- [ ] *2 onions - chop fine*
- [ ] *salt to taste*
- [ ] *1 tsp black pepper*
- [ ] *2 heaped tbsp flour*
- [ ] *2 small bunches coriander leaves - chop fine*
- [ ] *1 tbsp coriander (ketumbar) powder*
- [ ] *1 tsp chilli powder*
- [ ] *1/2 tsp turmeric powder*
- [ ] *oil for deep frying*

Method:

Combine all the ingredients, mix well, then shape into balls.

Heat oil, fry meat balls till golden brown.

Note: Beef or chicken may be used instead of mutton.

FRIED POTATOES

Ingredients:
- [ ] *450g small potatoes (if large ones are used, cut each into four) - peel and rub salt over them*
- [ ] *1 tbsp coriander (ketumbar) powder*
- [ ] *1/2 tbsp chilli powder*
- [ ] *1 tsp turmeric powder*
- [ ] *2 1/2 cups water*
- [ ] *6 tbsp ghee or cooking oil*
- [ ] *coriander leaves (for garnishing) - chop*

Method:

Heat ghee, and fry potatoes. When slightly brown, add coriander, chilli and turmeric powder and water.

Cover and cook until dry, stirring now and then during cooking.

When serving, garnish with chopped coriander leaves.

SLICED MUTTON CURRY WITH CAULIFLOWER

Ingredients:

- [ ] 450g lean mutton - cut into slices
- [ ] 4 small or 2 large tomatoes - cut into small cubes
- [ ] 1 medium sized onion - chop
- [ ] 2 1/2 tbsp water
- [ ] 2 tbsp coriander (ketumbar) powder
- [ ] 3 tsp chilli powder
- [ ] 1 tsp turmeric powder
- [ ] 1/2 tsp black pepper powder
- [ ] 3 sprigs coriander leaves - break into pieces
- [ ] a few mint leaves
- [ ] 10 almonds - scald, remove skin and grind fine
- [ ] 1 stick cinnamon - 4cm (1 1/2 in) long
- [ ] 2 cardamoms
- [ ] 3 cloves
- [ ] salt to taste
- [ ] 4 tbsp ghee or 8 tbsp cooking oil
- [ ] 2 cups water
- [ ] 230g cauliflower - cut into small florets

Method:

Combine mutton with all the ingredients (except cauliflower, ghee and 2 cups water) in a big bowl.

Heat ghee or oil. Put contents of bowl into oil and fry till fragrant. Add water, cover and cook, stirring now and then.

When meat is tender, add cauliflower and cook till gravy is fairly thick.

TOMATOCHICKEN CURRY

Ingredients:

- [ ] 1.75kg chicken - cut into medium sized pieces
- [ ] 2 pieces ginger - each the size of a walnut ⎫ grind to a
- [ ] 6 cloves garlic ⎭ fine paste
- [ ] 6 medium sized tomatoes - cut into very small cubes
- [ ] 2 medium sized onions - chop fine
- [ ] 4 level tbsp coriander (ketumbar) powder
- [ ] 2 level tbsp chilli powder
- [ ] 1 level tsp turmeric powder
- [ ] 5 sprigs coriander leaves - break into pieces
- [ ] 4 tbsp plain yoghurt
- [ ] salt to taste

In a big bowl, combine chicken with all the above ingredients

- [ ] 1 onion - slice thinly ⎫
- [ ] 4 cardamoms ⎬ ingredients
- [ ] 6 cloves ⎪ for frying
- [ ] 2 sticks cinnamon - each 3cm (1 1/2 in) long ⎭
- [ ] 8 level tbsp ghee
- [ ] 3 cups water
- [ ] 2 level tbsp tomato puree
- [ ] mint leaves - for garnishing

Method:

Heat ghee, add ingredients for frying and fry till fragrant. Add chicken, fry for about 5 minutes, then add water, cover pot and bring to the boil.

Mix tomato puree with a little water. When curry is boiling, add tomato puree and continue boiling till chicken is tender.

When serving garnish with mint leaves.

Mutton Curry with Cauliflower

TOMATO PUTCHREE

Ingredients:

- ☐ 1 tbsp cooking oil or ghee
- ☐ 6 medium sized tomatoes - cut each into 8 wedges
- ☐ 1 tsp chilli powder
- ☐ *$^1/_2$ tbsp coriander (ketumbar) powder*
- ☐ *$^1/_2$ tbsp turmeric powder*
- ☐ *$^1/_2$ cup water*
- ☐ 1 tbsp vinegar
- ☐ 1 tbsp sugar
- ☐ salt to taste
- ☐ 1 stick cinnamon - 4cm (1$^1/_2$ in) long ⎫
- ☐ 3 cloves garlic ⎬ *ingredients*
- ☐ 3 cardamoms ⎪ *for frying*
- ☐ *$^1/_2$ onion - slice finely* ⎭

Method:

Heat oil, add ingredients for frying and fry till fragrant. Add tomatoes and the rest of the ingredients and bring to the boil. Continue boiling for 1-2 minutes, then remove from heat.

Tomato Putchree

Fried Potatoes

Tomato Chicken Curry

Minced Mutton Balls

Pilau Rice with Cashew nuts

Fish Head Curry

Fried C

Crab Curry

80

South Indian Dishes

HOT PRAWN CURRY

Ingredients:
- [ ] *600g prawns (with shell)*
- [ ] *1 level tbsp chilli powder*
- [ ] *1 level tbsp coriander* (ketumbar) *powder*
- [ ] *1 tsp turmeric powder*
- [ ] *2 tsp black pepper powder* (reduce amount if milder flavour is required)
- [ ] *2 sprigs curry leaves* (karuvapillai)
- [ ] *salt to taste*
- [ ] *1 cup water*
- [ ] *1 big onion - thinly sliced*
- [ ] *4 tbsp cooking oil*

Method:

Put prawns in bowl. Add chilli, coriander, turmeric, black pepper powder, salt, 1 sprig curry leaves and water and leave for 10 minutes.

Heat oil, add sliced onion and the other sprig of curry leaves and fry till fragrant. Add marinated prawns and fry stirring now and then, until cooked.

Hot Prawn Curry

Rasam

FISH HEAD CURRY

Ingredients:

- [ ] 4 tbsp fish curry powder
- [ ] salt to taste
- [ ] 1 sprig curry leaves (karuvapillai)
- [ ] 1 red chilli
- [ ] 1 green chilli
- [ ] $1/_2$ onion - slice thick
- [ ] 1 clove garlic - slice
- [ ] 1 medium sized fresh tomato - to be used whole
- [ ] $1/_2$ cup water
- [ ] 2 tbsp tamarind - add 3 cups water, mix and strain to get tamarind juice
- [ ] 8-10 ladies fingers (okra) - slit lengthwise
- [ ] 1 medium sized fish head weighing about 900g - rub with salt and wash thoroughly
- [ ] 1 cup grated coconut (optional) - add $1/_2$ cup water and extract equal amount of milk
- [ ] 2 tsp fish curry spices (rempah tumis ikan) ⎫
- [ ] 1 sprig curry leaves   ⎬ ingredients to be fried
- [ ] 1 medium sized onion - slice thinly ⎭
- [ ] 3 tbsp cooking oil

Method:

Put curry powder, salt, curry leaves, chillies, onion, garlic and tomato in a medium sized bowl. Add water. Using a spoon or your hand, coarsely crush the chillies and tomato, then add tamarind juice to get a watery mixture. Set aside.

Heat oil, add ingredients to be fried and fry 1-2 seconds then add ladies fingers and fry till fragrant. Pour in curry mixture and keep pot covered till it is boiling. This is important to prevent the curry from tasting uncooked. Add fish head. If coconut milk is used, add when curry is boiling then bring back to the boil before adding fish head. Boil fish head till it is cooked.

RASAM

Ingredients:

- [ ] $1/_2$ tbsp black peppercorns ⎫
- [ ] $1/_2$ tbsp cumin (jintan puteh) ⎬ grind coarsely
- [ ] 4 cloves garlic - pound coarsely
- [ ] 1 tsp turmeric powder
- [ ] 1 tsp salt
- [ ] 1cm ($1/_2$in) cube of asafoetida
- [ ] 1 medium tomato
- [ ] 1 sprig curry leaves
- [ ] 1 tbsp tamarind - soak in some of the water from allowance and remove seeds
- [ ] $3^1/_2$ cups water
- [ ] 1 tbsp oil
- [ ] 2 dried chillies - break into pieces ⎫
- [ ] 1 small sprig curry leaves   ⎬
- [ ] $1/_2$ onion - finely sliced   ⎬ to be fried
- [ ] 1 tsp brown mustard seed   ⎭

Method:

In a large bowl, combine ground ingredients, garlic, turmeric, salt asafoetida, curry leaves, tamarind juice and water. Crush tomato in this then mix well. Heat oil in a deep pot, add ingredients to be fried. When brown add mixture in bowl to this. Cover pot and bring to boil. When steam emits from the pot, soup is ready. This soup may be served hot or cold.

Serve with deep fried papadom.

FRIED CABBAGE

Ingredients:

- [ ] 350-400g cabbage - shredded
- [ ] 2 green chillies - cut slantwise into fairly big pieces
- [ ] 1 big onion - slice thinly ⎫
- [ ] 1 sprig curry leaves (karuvapillai) ⎬ ingredients to be fried
- [ ] 1 tsp brown mustard seeds ⎬
- [ ] 1 tsp turmeric powder ⎭
- [ ] 1 cup grated coconut - add 1 cup water and extract equal amount of milk
- [ ] salt to taste
- [ ] 3 tbsp oil

Method:

Heat oil, add ingredients to be fried and chillies, and fry till fragrant. Add cabbage and stir fry for a few minutes. Add coconut milk and salt, and cook over medium heat till gravy boils. Continue cooking until cabbage is just tender then remove from heat.

CRAB CURRY

Ingredients:

- [ ] *600g crabs - cut body into two pieces*
- [ ] *1 tbsp coriander* (ketumbar) *powder*
- [ ] *1 level tsp cumin* (jintan puteh) *powder*
- [ ] *1 tbsp chilli powder*
- [ ] *1 tsp turmeric powder*
- [ ] *2 sprigs curry leaves* (karuvapillai)
- [ ] *1 onion - slice thick*
- [ ] *salt to taste*
- [ ] *1¹/₂ cups water*
- [ ] *4 tbsp oil*
- [ ] *1 tbsp rice - wash, drain and dry roast in dry pan till slightly brown then grind*

Method:

Put crabs in a large bowl; add coriander, cumin, chilli and turmeric powder, curry leaves, onion, salt and ¹/₂ cup water. Leave to stand for about 10 minutes.

Heat oil, add crabs and keep stirring. When crabs turn red add 1 cup water and simmer; when boiling, add ground rice to thicken gravy. Continue cooking, stirring all the time. When gravy is slightly thick remove from heat.

ROTI MARIAM

Ingredients:

- [ ] *450g plain flour - sieve*
- [ ] *2 eggs*
- [ ] *¹/₂ cup warm water mixed with 1 tsp salt*
- [ ] *2 tbsp ghee*
- [ ] *3 tbsp cooking oil*
- [ ] *oil for deep frying*

Method:

Put the flour, eggs, ghee and oil into a large bowl. Mix with the hand, then add water, a little at a time, to form a soft dough. Knead dough for about 10 minutes. Shape into lumps the size of a small potato.

On a lightly floured board, roll each lump into a round pancake, about 0.5cm (¹/₂ in) thick.

Deep fry the pancakes.

Serve with chicken or mutton curry.

CHICKEN COCONUT MILK CURRY

Ingredients:

- [ ] *1 chicken weighing approximately 1.5kg - cut into medium sized pieces*
- [ ] *¹/₂ medium sized onion - cut into thin wedge shaped slices*
- [ ] *1 green chilli* } *slash*
- [ ] *1 red chilli*
- [ ] *salt to taste*
- [ ] *4 sprigs big coriander leaves (optional) - cut into pieces*
- [ ] *³/₄ cup water*
- [ ] *10 slightly heaped tbsp meat curry powder*
- [ ] *1 piece ginger - size of walnut* } *grind to a fine paste*
- [ ] *4 cloves garlic*

In a big a bowl, combine chicken with all the above ingredients

- [ ] *¹/₂ onion - cut into thin slices*
- [ ] *1 stick cinnamon - 4cm (1¹/₂ in) long* } *ingredients for frying*
- [ ] *3 cardamoms*
- [ ] *3 cloves*
- [ ] *8 tbsp cooking oil*
- [ ] *3¹/₂ cups water*
- [ ] *10 small potatoes - peel and use whole*
- [ ] *1 cup grated coconut (optional) - add ¹/₂ cup water and extract equal amount of milk*

Method:

Heat oil, add ingredients for frying and fry till fragrant. Add chicken and fry till fragrant, then add water and potatoes and bring to the boil. Reduce heat and simmer. When potatoes are half cooked, add coconut milk and bring to the boil. Reduce heat and simmer until potatoes are cooked.

MUTTON CURRY

Ingredients:

- [ ] **900g mutton** - *cut into medium sized pieces*
- [ ] **6-8 cloves garlic** ⎫
- [ ] **3 slices ginger** - *each 1cm ($^1/_2$ in) thick* ⎬ *grind to fine paste*
- [ ] **1 red chilli** ⎫
- [ ] **1 green chilli** ⎬ *slash*
- [ ] **$^1/_2$ medium sized onion** - *cut into thick slices*
- [ ] **$^1/_2$ cup water**
- [ ] **2 tbsp plain yoghurt** *(optional)*
- [ ] **2 sprigs coriander leaves** - *break into pieces*
- [ ] **salt to taste**

In a large bowl, combine mutton with all the above ingredients.

- [ ] **1 stick cinnamon** - *3cm ($1^1/_4$ in) long* ⎫
- [ ] **$^1/_2$ medium sized onion** - *slice fine* ⎬ *ingredients*
- [ ] **4 cloves** ⎪ *for frying*
- [ ] **3 cardamoms** ⎭
- [ ] **4 tbsp oil**
- [ ] **4 cups water**
- [ ] **$1^1/_2$ tbsp tomato puree**
- [ ] **5-6 tomatoes** - *cut into wedges*

Curry mixture:

Mix the following with enough water to get a thick mixture:-

- [ ] **4 tbsp coriander** (ketumbar) *powder*
- [ ] **2 tbsp chilli powder**
- [ ] **$^1/_2$ tbsp cumin** (jintan puteh) *powder*
- [ ] **2 tsp turmeric powder**

Method:

Heat oil, add ingredients for frying. When fragrant, add mutton and stir fry a little, then add water. Bring to the boil, then simmer until meat is half cooked. Pour in curry mixture. Bring to the boil again, cover pot and simmer. Do not remove lid during this part of the cooking till fragrance emits from the pot. When gravy is quite thick, add tomato puree mixed with some of the gravy and continue cooking till meat is tender.

When almost cooked, add tomato wedges. Cook for a minute or two then remove from heat.

Serve with cucumber and tomato salad.

Salad

Roti Jala

Chicken Coconut Milk Curry

Mutton Curry

Roti Mariam

FRIED MUTTON CURRY

Ingredients:

- [ ] 450g mutton - cut into small cubes
- [ ] 6 level tbsp meat curry powder
- [ ] 4 cloves garlic
- [ ] 1 piece ginger (size of walnut) } grind to a fine paste
- [ ] salt to taste
- [ ] 8 tbsp oil

Ingredients for frying

- [ ] 1 onion - slice thinly
- [ ] 1 stick cinnamon - 4cm (1½ in) long
- [ ] 3 cardamoms
- [ ] 4 cloves
- [ ] 1 sprig curry leaves (karuvapillai)
- [ ] 2½ cups water
- [ ] 1 red chilli } cut in two lengthwise
- [ ] 1 green chilli
- [ ] 20 shallots - peel and use whole

Method:

In a large bowl, combine meat with curry powder, ginger-garlic paste and salt and mix well.

Heat oil and cook ingredients for frying till brown. Add meat and curry leaves, then stir fry till fragrant. Add water, cover pot and bring to the boil, then simmer, stirring now and then.

When gravy becomes fairly thick and meat is tender, add chillies and shallots. Stir for a few minutes, then remove from heat.

Fried Mutton Curry *South Indian Chicken C*

Crispy
Long Beans

Cuc
Sala

Indian Nasi Lemak

INDIAN NASI LEMAK

Ingredients:

- [ ] 600g Basmati rice - wash thoroughly and drain
- [ ] 2 tsp alba - soak, wash, drain and combine with clean rice
- [ ] 4 tbsp ghee
- [ ] ½ onion - slice thinly
- [ ] 1 stick cinnamon - 4cm (1½ in) long
- [ ] 2 cardamoms
- [ ] 3 cloves
- [ ] 2 fragrant screwpine leaves (daun pandan) - tie into a bundle
- [ ] 450g grated coconut - add 3 cups water and extract 3½ cups coconut milk
- [ ] salt to taste

Method:

Heat ghee in a large pot for cooking rice. Add onion, cinnamon, cardamoms, cloves and pandan leaves. Fry till onions are brown, then add coconut milk, rice and salt, stir. Cover pot and bring to the boil; when boiling, stir rice.

When rice is beginning to dry, lower heat and continue to cook. Keep the pot covered till the steam escapes, then uncover, turn rice over with a fork and cook for another 5-8 minutes.

Note: Indian Nasi Lemak, which is popular among South Indian Muslims, should be served with Chicken Curry, Cucumber Salad and Crispy Long Beans.

CUCUMBER SALAD

Ingredients:

- [ ] *2 cucumbers - peel, scrape design with fork and cut into slices of medium thickness*
- [ ] *salt to taste*
- [ ] *the juice of 3 small limes* (limau kesturi)
- [ ] *2 red chillies* } *slice thinly*
- [ ] *2 green chillies*
- [ ] *1 onion - cut into half and slice fine*
- [ ] *1 cup grated coconut - add $^1/_2$ cup water and extract $^3/_4$ cup milk*

Method:

Sprinkle salt over cucumber and leave for 5 minutes then rinse cucumber and drain.

Put the sliced cucumbers in a bowl, add lime juice, chillies and onion.

Pour coconut milk dressing over salad.

Note: If salad is to be kept, boil coconut milk dressing, cool, then pour over salad. If serving immediately, use freshly squeezed coconut milk.

CHICKEN CURRY

Ingredients:

- [ ] *1 chicken weighing about 1.75kg - wash and cut into medium sized pieces*
- [ ] *4 level tbsp meat curry powder*
- [ ] *salt to taste*
- [ ] *$^1/_2$ tsp black pepper powder*
- [ ] *1 sprig curry leaves* (karuvapillai)
- [ ] *4 level tbsp grated coconut - pound till fine*
- [ ] *6 tbsp oil*
- [ ] *2 cups water*
- [ ] *6 small potatoes - cut each in half*

Method:

Combine chicken with curry powder, salt, black pepper, curry leaves and coconut in a large bowl. Add $^1/_2$ cup water from allowance, then leave to marinate for about 10 minutes.

Heat oil, add chicken and stir fry till fragrant. Add the rest of the water and potatoes, cover and boil, stirring now and then. When potatoes are half cooked, reduce heat and let curry simmer. Remove from heat when potatoes are cooked and gravy a little thick.

CRISPY LONG BEANS

Ingredients:

- [ ] *300g long beans - cut into 3cm lengths*
- [ ] *1 sprig curry leaves* (karuvapillai)
- [ ] *1 level tsp turmeric powder*
- [ ] *1 level tsp chilli powder*
- [ ] *$1^1/_2$ tsp salt*
- [ ] *8 tbsp oil*

Method:

Put long beans in a bowl, sprinkle with turmeric, chilli powder and salt and mix thoroughly. Leave for 10-15 minutes.

Heat oil, fry curry leaves till crispy then add beans and stir fry from time to time. As beans start to get crisp, keep stirring constantly until the beans are very crisp. Remove from heat.

HOT KERALA CHICKEN CURRY

Ingredients:

- [ ] *$^1/_2$ chicken weighing about 750g - remove skin and cut into small pieces*
- [ ] *1 piece ginger 3cm ($1^1/_4$ in) long - slice fine*
- [ ] *$^1/_2$ tsp brown mustard seeds*
- [ ] *20 shallots - use whole*
- [ ] *1 sprig curry leaves* (karuvapillai)
- [ ] *salt to taste*
- [ ] *12 dried chillies* }
- [ ] *3 tbsp coriander* (ketumbar) *seeds* } *roast in dry pan then grind fine*
- [ ] *$^1/_2$ tsp cumin* (jintan puteh) *seeds*
- [ ] *$^1/_2$ tsp fennel* (jintan manis) *seeds*
- [ ] *1-2 tsp black peppercorns - grind fine*
- [ ] *5 tbsp oil*
- [ ] *1 cup water*

Method:

Combine chicken with ginger, mustard seeds, shallots, curry leaves, salt and all ground spices. Leave to marinate for about 10 minutes.

Heat oil, add chicken, fry till fragrant. Add water and simmer, keeping the pot covered. Stir once or twice during cooking. When gravy is a little thick, remove from heat.

Note: For this dish, the best flavour is obtained if the spices are ground in a batu giling (grinding stone).

Hot Kerala Chicken Curry

Carrots and Grated Coconut

Dhal Rasam

Sambal Ikan Bilis with Coconut

Fish Curry with Drumstick

FISH CURRY WITH DRUMSTICKS

Ingredients:

- [ ] *600g fish - ikan tenggiri or ikan kurau (Spanish mackerel, mulloway or any fish steaks) - cut into medium sized pieces*
- [ ] *5 drumsticks, peel and cut into 6cm (2 1/2 in) lengths*
- [ ] *2 tbsp coriander* (ketumbar) *seeds*
- [ ] *1 tsp fennel* (jintan manis) *seeds*
- [ ] *1/2 tsp black pepper corns*
- [ ] *1/2 tsp cumin* (jintan puteh) *seeds*
- [ ] *1 piece dried turmeric (size of almond)*
- [ ] *10 dried chillies*

soak for about an hour

- [ ] *2 sprigs curry leaves* (karuvapillai)
- [ ] *1 tsp fish curry spices* (rempah tumis ikan)
- [ ] *1/2 tbsp tamarind - mix with 1 1/2 cups water, strain to obtain juice*
- [ ] *salt to taste*
- [ ] *3 tbsp oil*

Method:

Grind soaked spices into a fine paste, adding chillies last. In a bowl, combine fish with curry paste, 1 sprig curry leaves and salt.

Heat oil, add 1 sprig curry leaves and fish curry spices, and fry till fragrant. Add fish and drumstick, fry till fragrant then add tamarind juice. Cover and bring to the boil over low heat.

When it has boiled, stir, cover again and cook for another 10 minutes.

CARROTS AND GRATED COCONUT

Ingredients:

- [ ] *300g carrots - peel, slice thinly and cut each slice in half*
- [ ] *1/2 cup grated coconut - grind*
- [ ] *1 tsp cumin* (jintan puteh) *powder*
- [ ] *2 tsp coriander* (ketumbar) *powder*
- [ ] *2 tsp turmeric powder*
- [ ] *1 tsp brown mustard seed*
- [ ] *1 sprig curry leaves* (karuvapillai)
- [ ] *salt to taste*
- [ ] *3/4 cup water*
- [ ] *5 tbsp oil*

Method:

Combine carrot with coconut, cumin, coriander and turmeric powder in a bowl.

Heat oil, add mustard seeds and curry leaves, and fry till fragrant.

Add carrots, fry till fragrant, then add water and continue cooking till carrots are soft and the consistency slightly wet.

DHAL RASAM

Ingredients:

- [ ] *60g yellow lentils* (dhal) *- soak for about 3 hours, then wash, remove stones and skin, and drain*
- [ ] *6 cups water*
- [ ] *1 tsp black peppercorns - grind coarsely*
- [ ] *a very small piece of asafoetida - about the size of large pea*
- [ ] *1/2 tsp brown mustard seed (optional)*
- [ ] *1 sprig curry leaves* (karuvapillai)
- [ ] *salt to taste*

Method:

Put dhal and water in a saucepan and boil for about 1/2 an hour. Drain dhal and put aside for use in another recipe. Put water back into saucepan, add pepper, asafoetida, mustard seeds, curry leaves and salt and bring back to the boil.

Continue boiling for another 5 minutes.

Serve hot or cold.

Note: The boiled dhal left over may be mixed with sugar and grated coconut and eaten as a sweet.

SAMBAL IKAN BILIS WITH COCONUT

Ingredients:
- ☐ 40g dried anchovies (ikan bilis) - split in half
- ☐ 1 cup grated coconut
- ☐ 5 shallots
- ☐ 3 red chillies
- ☐ 1 piece ginger (size of almond)
- ☐ 1 tsp tamarind - remove seeds
- ☐ salt to taste
- ☐ oil for deep frying

Method:
Deep fry ikan bilis till crisp, then drain.

Grind coconut, add tamarind pulp and salt and continue grinding till fine. Add chillies, shallots and ginger and when fine, add fried ikan bilis and grind coarsely. Put paste in serving dish.

TOMATO RICE

Ingredients:
- ☐ 600g Basmati rice - wash and drain
- ☐ water - equal in volume to rice used
- ☐ 3 cloves garlic ⎱ grind to a
- ☐ 2 slices ginger (each 2cm or $^3/_4$ in thick) ⎰ smooth paste
- ☐ $^1/_2$ onion - thinly sliced
- ☐ 1 piece cinnamon 5cm (2 in) in length ⎱ ingredients for
- ☐ 4 cloves ⎰ frying
- ☐ 3 cardamoms
- ☐ 1 fragrant screwpine leaf (daun pandan)
- ☐ 1 tin tomato juice (approx. 1 cup)
- ☐ 1 tbsp plain yoghurt
- ☐ 2 tbsp evaporated milk
- ☐ 4 tbsp ghee
- ☐ salt to taste

Method:
Mix tomato juice and yoghurt with water and milk. Heat ghee, add ingredients for frying, garlic-ginger paste and pandan leaf. When onions are brown, add tomato-water-milk mixture and salt. Cover pot and bring to the boil. Add rice.

When water is absorbed, lower heat and continue cooking, making quite sure the pot is well covered. When steam emits from pot, the rice is cooked. When serving, garnish rice with green peas and shredded omelette.

Note: The cooking takes about 45 minutes
This amount of rice will serve 6-8 people

PINEAPPLE PUTCHREE

Ingredients:
- ☐ 1 medium sized almost-ripe pineapple - peel, quarter, remove hard core, then cut into wedges about 1cm ($^1/_2$ in) thick
- ☐ 3 tsp turmeric powder
- ☐ 3 red chillies ⎱ slit lengthwise
- ☐ 3 green chillies ⎰
- ☐ 5 tbsp sugar
- ☐ 1 stick cinnamon 6cm (2 $^1/_2$ in) ⎱
- ☐ 4 cardamoms ⎟ ingredients for
- ☐ 6 cloves ⎟ frying
- ☐ 1 onion - slice thinly ⎰
- ☐ 1 piece ginger (size of walnut) - slice thinly and cut into matchstick lengths
- ☐ 4 tbsp oil
- ☐ salt

Method:
Bring pineapple to the boil with turmeric powder, then cook for 10 minutes. Remove from heat and drain. Discard water.

Heat oil, add ingredients to be fried. Fry till fragrant, add pineapple, sugar, chillies and a pinch of salt stirring after each addition. Continue to cook for another 5 minutes.

MYSORE FRIED CHICKEN

Ingredients:
- ☐ $1^1/_2$ kg chicken - remove skin and cut into small pieces
- ☐ 2 onions - cut into half and slice thinly
- ☐ 2 green chillies ⎱ cut into thin strips
- ☐ 1 red chilli ⎰
- ☐ 2 tbsp coriander (ketumbar) powder
- ☐ 1 tbsp chilli powder
- ☐ 1 tsp turmeric powder
- ☐ salt to taste
- ☐ 10 stalks big coriander leaves - chop
- ☐ 2 cups water
- ☐ 8 tbsp oil

Method:
Combine chicken with all the above ingredients (except oil) and 1 cup water from allowance in a big bowl. Heat oil, add chicken, fry till fragrant. Add rest of water, cover and leave to boil over a low heat until chicken is dry and brown, stirring occasionally. Garnish with small coriander leaves and potato crisps.

Tomato Rice

Beef Samak

Pineapple Putchree

Mysore Fried Chicken

91

Sothi

Salt Fish Curry

Fried Spinach

Fried Long Beans with
Grated Coconut

SOTHI

Ingredients:

- [ ] 450g grated coconut - add 2 cups water and extract an equal amount of milk
- [ ] ½ tsp turmeric powder
- [ ] 1 sprig curry leaves (karuvapillai)
- [ ] 1 tbsp tamarind - mix with a little of the coconut milk and strain
- [ ] ½ tsp fenugreek (alba)
- [ ] 1 green chilli
- [ ] 1 tomato
- [ ] ½ onion - slice thinly
- [ ] 1 small sprig curry leaves (karuvapillai) ⎫ ingredients
- [ ] 3 dried chillies - break each into 3 pieces ⎬ for frying
- [ ] 2 tbsp oil

Method:

Combine coconut milk, turmeric powder, curry leaves, tamarind juice and fenugreek in a pot. Using your hand or a spoon, crush the tomato and the chilli in the coconut milk. Bring to the boil stirring all the time. When boiling remove from heat.

Heat oil, add ingredients to be fried. When onions are brown, add the fried ingredients to the cooked Sothi and cover for a moment, then remove cover. Stir, then keep covered till ready to serve.

BEEF SAMAK

Ingredients:

- [ ] 300g topside beef or round steak - cut into two pieces
- [ ] 2 medium sized tomatoes - slice thinly
- [ ] 1 slice ginger 2.5cm (1 in) thick ⎫
- [ ] 4 cloves garlic ⎬ grind to a fine paste
- [ ] 8 dried chillies - soak to soften ⎭
- [ ] 1 tsp coriander (ketumbar) powder
- [ ] 1 tsp cumin (jintan puteh) powder
- [ ] ½ tsp white pepper powder
- [ ] 1 tbsp plain yoghurt
- [ ] 1 cup water
- [ ] 2 tsp tomato puree - mix with a little water
- [ ] 6 tbsp oil
- [ ] salt to taste
- [ ] 1 small onion - slice thinly ⎫
- [ ] 1 stick cinnamon 3cm (1¼ in) length ⎬ ingredients
- [ ] 3 cloves ⎪ for frying
- [ ] 3 cardamoms ⎭
- [ ] 2 tbsp cooked peas

Method:

In a bowl, combine beef with sliced tomatoes, ground ingredients, coriander, cumin and pepper powder, yoghurt and salt.

Heat oil, add ingredients for frying. Fry till onions are brown then add beef and fry till fragrant. Add water, cover and boil. When meat is tender, add puree, stir and cook for another 10 minutes. Gravy should be of a thick consistency.

Garnish with cooked green peas.

FRIED LONG BEANS WITH GRATED COCONUT

Ingredients:

- [ ] 2 tbsp oil
- [ ] ½ onion - slice thinly
- [ ] 1 green chilli - slice diagonally
- [ ] 1 tsp turmeric powder
- [ ] 1 small sprig curry leaves (karuvapillai)
- [ ] ½ tsp brown mustard seeds
- [ ] ½ cup grated coconut - grind coarsely
- [ ] salt to taste
- [ ] ½ teacup water
- [ ] 300g long beans - cut into 2cm (¾ in) lengths

Method:

Heat oil in frying pan and fry onion, chilli, turmeric powder, curry leaves and mustard seeds till light brown. Add ground coconut and salt and keep frying till fragrant. Add water, stir, then add long beans and cook till beans are tender stirring now and then while cooking.

SALT FISH CURRY

Ingredients:
- [ ] 150g salted Ikan Kurau meat (or dried salted cod)
  - cut into pieces 2cm ($^3/_4$ in) thick, soak for a few minutes and wash
- [ ] 230g salted Ikan Kurau bones - cut into 2
- [ ] 10-12 small potatoes - wash skin thoroughly; do not peel
- [ ] 3 purple eggplant (brinjal) - cut each in half lengthwise then cut each half into 3 pieces
- [ ] 4 drumsticks - peel and cut into 6cm ($2^1/_2$ in) lengths
- [ ] 8 long beans - break or cut into 5cm (2 in) lengths
- [ ] 8 tbsp oil
- [ ] 8 medium sized tomatoes - cut in half

Combine in a large bowl:
- [ ] 10 tbsp fish curry powder
- [ ] 2 tbsp grated coconut - grind into a fine paste
- [ ] 2 green chillies ⎫
- [ ] 1 red chilli ⎭ break into 3 pieces
- [ ] 1 sprig curry leaves (karuvapillai)
- [ ] $^1/_2$ onion - slice thickly
- [ ] 2 tbsp tamarind - mix with 3 cups water and strain to get tamarind juice
- [ ] 2 cloves garlic - slice thickly
- [ ] salt to taste
- [ ] 1 whole tomato - crush

Ingredients for frying:
- [ ] $^1/_2$ onion - slice finely
- [ ] 1 tbsp fish curry spices (rempah tumis ikan)
- [ ] 1 small sprig curry leaves (karuvapillai)

Method:
Heat oil, add ingredients for frying. When fragrant, add potatoes and fry for 5 minutes. Add ingredients which have been combined, brinjal, long beans and drumsticks. Cover, bring to the boil and continue boiling till potatoes are nearly cooked. Add salt fish and bones, reduce heat and cook for another 10 minutes. Add tomato halves, leave for a minute then remove from heat.

Note: If mangoes are available, add 2 green mangoes, cut into small pieces, together with the other vegetables. Reduce amount of tamarind if mango is used. No salt is needed for this curry as the salt fish will give it sufficient taste.

Note: Serve with deep fried chilli tairu available from any Indian spice shop.

FRIED SPINACH

Ingredients:
- [ ] 300g spinach - chop off roots, wash and cut fine
- [ ] 450g grated coconut - add 1 cup water to get an equal amount of milk
- [ ] $^1/_2$ onion - slice thinly ⎫
- [ ] 1 green chilli - cut slantwise into 5-6 pieces ⎪
- [ ] $^1/_2$ tsp brown mustard seeds ⎪
- [ ] $^1/_2$ tsp turmeric powder ⎬ ingredients for frying
- [ ] 1 tsp cumin (jintan puteh) powder ⎪
- [ ] $^1/_2$ tsp chilli powder ⎪
- [ ] 3-4 curry leaves (karuvapillai) ⎭
- [ ] 2 tbsp oil
- [ ] salt to taste

Method:
Heat oil, add ingredients for frying. Fry till onions are a light brown then add spinach and stir to mix it with the spices. Add coconut milk and salt and allow to cook, stirring now and then. When spinach is soft and a little gravy is left, remove from heat.

SPICY FRIED MUTTON

Ingredients:
- [ ] 450g mutton - cut into small cubes
- [ ] 2 green chillies ⎫
- [ ] 2 red chillies ⎭ cut into thin strips lengthwise
- [ ] 1 onion - cut into half, then slice thinly
- [ ] 3 tbsp meat curry powder
- [ ] salt to taste
- [ ] 1 sprig curry leaves (karuvapillai) - use leaves only
- [ ] $^1/_2$ cup water
- [ ] 5 tbsp oil
- [ ] 2 cups water

Method:
Combine mutton with all the above ingredients in a bowl (except oil and 2 cups water)

Heat oil, add mutton and fry till fragrant. Add water, cover and bring to the boil, then continue boiling, stirring now and then.

Lower heat when the amount of liquid is reduced. When curry is almost dry, remove from heat.

Garnish with potato crisps or small coriander leaves.

Nasi Briani

PICKLE

Ingredients:

- [ ] *1 large or 2 medium cucumbers - cut into 5 cm (2in) strips, discarding the pulp*
- [ ] *1 large carrot - peel and cut into 5 cm (2 in) strips*
- [ ] *30 small round shallots - peel*
- [ ] *5 green chillies* ⎫
- [ ] *5 red chillies* ⎬ *slash*
- [ ] *5 slices ginger, each 1cm ($\frac{1}{2}$ in) thick - shred*
- [ ] *20 small cloves garlic*
- [ ] *2 tsp chilli powder* ⎫
- [ ] *1 tsp turmeric powder* ⎬ *add sufficient water*
- [ ] *1 $\frac{1}{2}$ tsp brown mustard seed* ⎭ *to make a paste*
- [ ] *3 tbsp oil*
- [ ] *$\frac{1}{4}$ cup water*
- [ ] *3 tbsp vinegar*
- [ ] *2 tbsp sugar*
- [ ] *salt to taste*

Method:

Sprinkle salt generously over cucumber, carrot, ginger, chilli, shallots and garlic and leave in the sun for a few hours, turning vegetables over now and then. Get rid of excess moisture.

Heat oil, add chilli-turmeric paste and fry. Add water, vinegar, sugar and salt and stir till sugar dissolves. Add the vegetables, stir for about 5 minutes then remove from heat. Do not overcook or vegetables will not be crisp.

Dalcha

Spicy Fried Mutton

Pickle

Lime Pickle

INDIAN DALCHA

Ingredients:

- [ ] 450g mutton ribs - cut into medium sized pieces
- [ ] 1 cup yellow lentils (dhal) - soak in water for 2-3 hours
- [ ] 3 slices ginger - each 1cm ($^1/_2$ in) thick } grind to a
- [ ] 4 cloves garlic } smooth paste
- [ ] $^1/_2$ big onion - slice thick
- [ ] 2 green chillies } slit half way
- [ ] 1 red chilli }
- [ ] $1^1/_2$ level tsp turmeric powder
- [ ] 1 sprig curry leaves (karuvapillai)
- [ ] 1 stick cinnamon - 3cm ($1^1/_4$ in) long
- [ ] 2 cardamoms
- [ ] 3 cloves
- [ ] salt to taste
- [ ] 8 cups water
- [ ] 300g small potatoes - peel and cut into half
- [ ] 2 bananas (pisang kari) - split in half and cut each half into 3-4 pieces
- [ ] 3 carrots - cut into 4 cm ($1^1/_2$ in) lengths
- [ ] 3 purple eggplants (brinjals) - split in half then cut each half into 3-4 pieces
- [ ] 1 green mango - cut into 3 pieces
- [ ] 2 tbsp meat curry powder - add 8 tbsp water to make watery mixture
- [ ] 1 cup grated coconut - add $^3/_4$ cup water and extract equal amount of thick coconut milk
- [ ] $1^1/_2$ tbsp tamarind - mix with coconut milk and strain
- [ ] 300g tomatoes - cut into half
- [ ] 6 tsp oil
- [ ] 1 bunch small coriander leaves for garnishing
- [ ] 1 big onion - slice thinly
- [ ] 1 tbsp chilli powder } ingredients for frying
- [ ] 1 sprig curry leaves (karuvapillai) }

Method:

Put mutton in a deep pot together with dhal, ginger-garlic paste, thickly sliced onion, green and red chillies, turmeric powder, curry leaves, cinnamon, cardamoms, cloves and salt. Add water and boil until meat and dhal are cooked.

Add potatoes, bananas, carrots, brinjal, mango and curry powder mixture, cover pot and boil. Do not uncover until it has boiled for 5 minutes.

Add coconut milk which has been mixed with tamarind and cover pot again. Do not uncover until curry is boiling and the vegetables are cooked.

Add tomatoes and leave for 1 or 2 seconds only, then remove from heat.

Heat oil in frying pan and cook ingredients for frying till golden brown. Pour contents of pan (including oil) into the pot of Dalcha and cover immediately. When serving, garnish the Dalcha with a few small coriander leaves.

Note: For a hot Dalcha, add more chilli powder when you fry the sliced onions and curry leaves.

If mango is not used, increase amount of tamarind to 2 tablespoons.

NASI BRIANI

Ingredients:

- [ ] 1 chicken weighing approximately 1.5kg - cut chicken into 4 pieces, wash and drain
- [ ] 4 slices ginger - each 1 cm ($^1/_2$ in) thick } grind to a
- [ ] 4 cloves garlic } smooth paste
- [ ] 1 red chilli } slit halfway
- [ ] 1 green chilli }
- [ ] 4 small tomatoes - slice
- [ ] 3 tbsp (slightly heaped) meat curry powder
- [ ] 2 small bunches big coriander leaves - chop coarsely
- [ ] a small bunch mint leaves
- [ ] 4 tbsp plain yoghurt
- [ ] 1 tsp pepper
- [ ] salt to taste
- [ ] $1^1/_2$ cups water
- [ ] 10 tbsp ghee
- [ ] 1 big onion - slice thinly }
- [ ] 1 stick cinnamon - 4cm ($1^1/_2$ in) long } ingredients
- [ ] 4 cloves } for frying
- [ ] 4 cardamoms }
- [ ] 6 almonds - scald and remove skin } grind fine
- [ ] 6 cashew nuts }
- [ ] $1^1/_2$ tbsp tomato paste
- [ ] 2 medium sized onions - slice thinly and fry till golden brown
- [ ] 2 tsp briani spices (see glossary)
- [ ] 120g cashew nuts - fry till golden brown and keep aside for garnishing
- [ ] 1 bunch of small coriander leaves for garnishing

Ingredients for rice:

- [ ] 600g Basmati rice
- [ ] 1 small tin evaporated milk
- [ ] 2 tsp yellow food colouring
- [ ] 3 tsp rose water (ayer mawar)

Method of preparing chicken:

Combine chicken with garlic-ginger paste, chillies, tomatoes, meat curry powder, big coriander leaves, mint leaves, yoghurt, pepper, salt and $^1/_2$ cup water from allowance

Heat ghee in a pot then add ingredients for frying and fry till golden brown. Add chicken and fry for a little while, turning it over a few times. Add 1 cup water and bring to the boil.

When boiling, lower heat, add ground almond and cashew nuts, tomato paste, fried onion slices and briani spices. Turn over the chicken pieces, then leave to simmer till almost dry. Remove chicken from the pot and set aside. Pour left-over ghee into a bowl and leave to cool. This pot will be used for cooking the rice.

Method of preparing rice:

Bring $\frac{3}{4}$ of a large saucepan of slightly salted water to boil. Wash and drain rice.

When water is boiling, put in the rice and boil till it is almost cooked.

When rice is almost cooked, remove from heat and drain off water. Mix evaporated milk with the ghee left over from cooking chicken.

Into the pot used to cook chicken, put a layer of rice then a layer of chicken. Repeat till chicken and rice are used up, making sure that rice forms the last layer. Pour the oil-milk mixture over the rice.

Mix rose water with yellow colouring and sprinkle over rice. Scatter a few mint leaves over rice.

Cook over low heat making sure the pot is well covered till steam emits from pot. Do not uncover pot while rice is cooking.

When serving, garnish rice with fried cashew nuts and small coriander leaves.

LIME PICKLE

Ingredients:

- [ ] *2 limes (commercially bottled Indian Lime Pickle) - chop*
- [ ] *1 large onion - cut in half and slice fine*
- [ ] *1 red chilli* } *slice fine (remove seeds*
- [ ] *2 green chillies* } *for mild flavour)*

Method:

Combine all the above ingredients in a bowl, mix well and put in serving dish.

CHICKEN KEBAB

Ingredients:

- [ ] *600g chicken - debone and cut meat into small cubes*

Grind to a fine paste:

- [ ] *1 tsp cumin (jintan puteh) seeds* } *soak for ¹/₂ hour*
- [ ] *1 tsp black peppercorns*
- [ ] *2 slices ginger - each 1cm (¹/₂ in) thick*
- [ ] *3 cloves garlic*
- [ ] *2 red chillies*

- [ ] *1 tsp coriander (ketumbar) powder*
- [ ] *salt to taste*
- [ ] *1 tbsp plain yoghurt or juice of ¹/₂ lemon*
- [ ] *3 tbsp oil*

Method:

Combine ground ingredients, coriander powder, salt and yoghurt or lemon juice with chicken. Leave to marinate for about 10 minutes.

Heat oil, add chicken and cook till chicken is tender and fairly dry.

Alternatively, put marinated chicken on a tray, brush with oil and grill.

To serve:

Put chicken pieces with pickled onions through cocktail sticks or little skewers.

Tahu Balls

Fried Ikan Bilis

Green Chilli Sauce

Pakora

Vegetable Puffs

Samosa

Satay Flavoured Fish Balls

Chicken Kebab

Murukku

Spicy Squids

Spicy Prawn Fritters

99

VEGETABLE PUFFS
(Epok-Epok Sayur)

Ingredients for filling:
- [ ] 1 clove garlic ⎫
- [ ] 2 red chillies ⎬ *grind to a fine paste*
- [ ] 4 shallots ⎭
- [ ] 150g shrimps - *remove shell, cut into small pieces*
- [ ] 300g bean sprouts - *remove tails*
- [ ] 10 sprigs coarse chives (kuchai) - *chop fine*
- [ ] 2 hard beancurd (taukwa) - *deep fry till a light brown then cut into small cubes*
- [ ] salt to taste
- [ ] 2 tbsp oil

Ingredients for pastry:
- [ ] 340g plain flour
- [ ] 5 tbsp cooking oil
- [ ] $1/4$ cup water - *mix with a little salt*

Method for filling:
Heat oil, add ground ingredients and salt and fry till fragrant. Add shrimps, fry for a minute or two, then add bean sprouts and kuchai. Stir for a few minutes. Finally, add taukwa and stir, mixing vegetables well. Remove from heat, drain and cool.

Method for pastry:
Sieve flour into bowl, add oil and work it into the flour, adding just enough water to form a dough. Knead for about 5 minutes.

Roll out half the pastry at a time to 3mm ($1/8$ in) thick. Use a 6cm ($2^1/2$ in) cutter to cut pastry into rounds.

Put a scant teaspoon of filling in each round. Damp edges of pastry with water, bring together, seal tightly and flute edges.

Deep fry till golden brown.

Serve with chilli sauce.

FRIED IKAN BILIS

Ingredients:
- [ ] 150g dried anchovies (ikan bilis) - *remove head and slash each halfway down; do not wash*
- [ ] oil for deep frying
- [ ] 15 dried chillies - *soak and grind to a fine paste*
- [ ] 3 tsp sugar
- [ ] salt to taste
- [ ] 2 tsp local vinegar

Method:
Heat oil, add ikan bilis and deep fry till crisp. Remove and drain.

Leave 8 tbsp oil in pan. Heat, add ground chillies and fry, then add sugar and salt and continue frying for a few minutes. Add vinegar and keep frying till mixture is fairly thick and well cooked. Add ikan bilis, stir, mixing well with chilli mixture. When thoroughly mixed, remove and put the ikan bilis in a strainer to drain off excess oil.

SPICY SQUIDS

Ingredients:
- [ ] 600g small to medium sized squids (sotong) - *clean well*
- [ ] 2 tsp black peppercorns - *grind fine*
- [ ] $1^1/2$ tsp turmeric powder
- [ ] salt to taste
- [ ] 3 tsp water
- [ ] 8 tbsp oil

Method:
Mix black pepper, turmeric powder and water and fry in oil until fragrant.

Add cuttlefish and salt and fry for about 5 minutes. Remove and drain.

GREEN CHILLI SAUCE

Ingredients:
- [ ] 3 green chillies
- [ ] 1 clove garlic
- [ ] 4 sprigs coriander leaves
- [ ] 2-3 limes
- [ ] salt to taste

Method:
Cut up chilli, garlic and coriander leaves. Grind all till fine. Put ground chilli in dish, add lime juice and salt. Mix well.

SATAY FLAVOURED FISH BALLS

Ingredients:
- [ ] 30 small fish balls

Grind to a paste: (neither too fine nor too coarse)
- [ ] 3 dried chillies - soak beforehand
- [ ] 1 stalk lemon grass (serai)
- [ ] 1 slice lengkuas - 1cm ($^1/_2$in) thick
- [ ] 5 shallots
- [ ] 1 clove garlic
- [ ] 1 small piece dried turmeric - size of almond
- [ ] 1 tbsp coriander (ketumbar) seeds
- [ ] $^1/_2$ tsp fennel (jintan manis) seeds
- [ ] $^1/_2$ tsp cumin (jintan puteh) seeds

- [ ] 1 tsp tamarind ⎱ mix and strain to obtain juice
- [ ] 1 tsp water ⎰
- [ ] 1 tbsp sugar
- [ ] salt to taste
- [ ] 2 tbsp oil

Method:
Heat oil, then add ground ingredients and tamarind juice and fry till fragrant. Add sugar and salt and cook for a minute or two till sugar dissolves. Add fish balls. Mix well with spices.

TAHU BALLS

Ingredients:
- [ ] 1 taukwa - mash with fork
- [ ] 1 small carrot - peel and chop fine
- [ ] 2 stalks coriander leaves ⎫
- [ ] 1 stalk spring onion ⎬ chop fine
- [ ] 1 red chilli ⎭
- [ ] $^1/_4$ tsp pepper
- [ ] salt to taste
- [ ] 1 egg (use half in mixture and half to dip tahu balls into)
- [ ] plain flour
- [ ] oil for deep frying

Method:
Combine taukwa, carrot, chopped coriander leaves, spring onion, chilli, pepper, salt and half an egg. Mix well. Shape into balls. Dip tahu balls in beaten egg then flour and deep fry in hot oil till golden brown.

SPICY PRAWN FRITTERS

Ingredients:
- [ ] 600g medium sized prawns - remove shell but keep tails
- [ ] 3 slightly heaped tbsp rice flour
- [ ] salt to taste
- [ ] $2^1/_2$ tbsp water
- [ ] oil for deep frying

Ingredients for gravy:
- [ ] 1 clove garlic ⎫
- [ ] 1 piece ginger - size of almond ⎬ grind to a fine paste
- [ ] 15 dried chillies - soak beforehand ⎭
- [ ] 4 tbsp oil
- [ ] 3 tsp sugar
- [ ] salt to taste
- [ ] 2 tsp light soya sauce
- [ ] 2 tsp vinegar

Method:
Put flour and salt in a bowl and mix with water to make a batter.

Add prawns to mixture.

Heat oil, add prawns and fry. Remove as soon as fritters are lightly brown and keep aside.

Method for gravy:
Heat oil, add ground ingredients and fry. Add sugar and salt, stir, then add soya sauce and vinegar. Continue stirring until gravy is fairly thick, then add fried prawn fritters and stir, mixing well with chilli mixture. Remove from heat as soon as fritters are well covered with gravy.

SAMOSAS

Ingredients for filling:
- [ ] 300g minced beef
- [ ] ¹/₂ cup water
- [ ] salt to taste
- [ ] 1 tsp pepper
- [ ] 5 cloves garlic
- [ ] 5 green chillies
- [ ] 2 red chillies
- [ ] ginger - 1 piece measuring 3x2x1 cm

} grind to a fine paste

- [ ] 3 onions - either grate fine or cut into small squares
- [ ] 1 tsp coriander (ketumbar) powder
- [ ] ¹/₂ tsp chilli powder
- [ ] ¹/₂ tsp turmeric powder
- [ ] 4-5 sprigs big coriander leaves - chop fine
- [ ] 1 small bunch mint - chop fine

Ingredients for pastry:
- [ ] 340g plain flour
- [ ] a pinch of baking powder
- [ ] 120g margarine
- [ ] water

Method for filling:
Combine minced beef, water, salt, pepper and chilli-garlic-ginger paste in a saucepan and boil till almost dry. Add chopped onions, coriander, chilli and turmeric powder, stir and remove from heat. Add chopped mint and coriander leaves, mix and leave to cool.

Method for pastry:
Sieve flour and baking powder into a bowl.

Melt the margarine and when cool, work into flour.

Add a little water at a time, using just enough to form a dough. Knead so that pastry becomes elastic.

Divide pastry into little lumps of equal size. Take 1 lump, roll it paper thin into a circle, dusting with flour to make rolling easier.

Cut each circle in half, place a spoonful of cooked meat mixture on each semi-circle; fold pastry over to form a triangle, moisten edges and seal carefully. Repeat till all the pastry is used.

Heat sufficient oil for deep frying and fry the samosas over moderate heat till golden brown. Drain and serve with chilli sauce, mint sauce or yoghurt.

Note: Size of samosas may vary; for cocktails, however, small ones are preferable.

Instead of making your own pastry, spring roll pastry (poh piah skin) may be used. Cut pastry squares into strips (6cm width). Put filling and fold to form a triangle.

CHILLI PAKORHAS
(Chilli Fritters)

Ingredients:
- [ ] 6-8 green chillies - to be used whole.
  (select ones with a short stem)
- [ ] 4 tbsp besan (chick pea flour)
- [ ] 1 tsp coriander powder
- [ ] ¹/₂ tsp cumin powder
- [ ] ¹/₂ tsp turmeric powder
- [ ] salt to taste
- [ ] about ¹/₃ cup water
- [ ] oil for deep frying

Method:
In a bowl, put besan, spice powders and salt. Mix. Add water, a little at a time. Stir to blend then beat till smooth. Consistency of batter should be neither too thick nor too thin. Adjust water quantity accordingly.

Heat oil. Dip chilli in batter shaking off excess and fry in hot oil. When brown, remove and drain on absorbent paper.

SINDHI SANDWICH

Ingredients for filling:
- [ ] 2 soft boiled eggs (3 mins) - shell
- [ ] 1 onion - slice fine
- [ ] 2 green chillies - slash into 4 lengthwise and chop
- [ ] 40g grated cheddar cheese (or chop 2 slices SINGLES)
- [ ] 1 tomato - remove seeds, chop fine
- [ ] 2 sprigs coriander leaves - chop fine
- [ ] 12 slices of sandwich bread

Method:
Put eggs in a bowl and mash with fork. Add the rest of the above ingredients and a dash of black pepper. Mix well.

Spread slices of bread thinly with margarine or butter.

Spread filling on 6 slices and cover with the other 6 slices.

Cut each sandwich into triangles or fingers.

CHICKEN SALAD SANDWICH (ARAB)

Ingredients for filling:

- [ ] *1 chicken thigh or 200g chicken breast*
  - de-bone and chop meat
- [ ] *1 tsp turmeric powder (kunyit)* } *add to chopped chicken*
- [ ] *1/2 tsp black pepper powder*
- [ ] *1 tbsp butter or margarine*
- [ ] *Juice of 2 limes*
- [ ] *1 small carrot - cut into fine strips*
- [ ] *2 tomatoes - chop*
- [ ] *3 lettuce leaves - shred*
- [ ] *8 hot dog rolls*

Method:

Heat butter, add chicken and fry. Sprinkle with a little water and continue frying. When almost cooked, add lime juice. When chicken is dry, add carrot and tomato, stir, cook a little then remove from heat.

Slash each roll, put in a quantity of cooked filling and shredded lettuce. Cut each roll in half or in 3 sections.

SALATA
(Salad Sandwich)

Ingredients:

- [ ] *1/4 lettuce - shred*
- [ ] *2 tomatoes - remove seeds and cut into strips*
- [ ] *4 tbsp pickled cabbage/carrot (see recipe for Roast Beef and Pickle Sandwich)*
- [ ] *6-8 slices of sandwich bread*

Method:

Mix all the above ingredients in a bowl.
Spread a thin layer of butter or margarine on slices of bread.
Use filling to make sandwiches.

ROAST BEEF AND PICKLE SANDWICH

Ingredients:

For pickle:
- [ ] *200g cabbage - shred*
- [ ] *100g carrot - peel and cut into fine strips*
- [ ] *1/4 cup white vinegar*
- [ ] *2 tbsp sugar*

Method:

Heat vinegar, sugar and a dash of salt. When sugar has dissolved, boil for a while. Cool the vinegar before adding cabbage and carrot. (This pickle can be prepared a day before)

For filling:

- [ ] *1 tbsp butter or margarine*
- [ ] *4 thin slices of beef fillet (approx. 150g) - shred*
- [ ] *1/2 tsp black pepper* } *add to beef*
- [ ] *salt to taste*
- [ ] *1 tomato*
- [ ] *2 onions* } *chop*
- [ ] *1 stalk coriander leaves*
- [ ] *8-10 hot dog rolls or hamburger buns*

Method:

Heat butter, add beef. Fry till almost dry. Turn off heat, stir in tomato, onion and coriander leaves.

Slash rolls or buns, fill with beef mixture and some pickled vegetable.

SPICY SCRAMBLED EGG SANDWICH

Ingredients:

- ☐ 4 eggs - beat and add a little salt
- ☐ 2 red chillies
- ☐ 1 clove garlic } grind
- ☐ 2 tbsp oil
- ☐ cucumber and tomato slices
- ☐ 12 slices of sandwich bread

Method:

Heat a little oil, pour in eggs and cook, stirring to scramble it. When cooked but still moist, remove from heat.

Heat 2 tbsp oil, add ground ingredients. When fragrant, add scrambled egg. Mix well and remove from heat.

Spread filling on 6 slices of bread, cover with the other six slices. Cut into triangles or fingers.

Spicy Scrambled Egg

Sindhi

Salata

Chicken Salad

Roast Beef and Pickle

105

Serikaya Beras

Ondeh Ondeh Keledek

Ubi Cerah

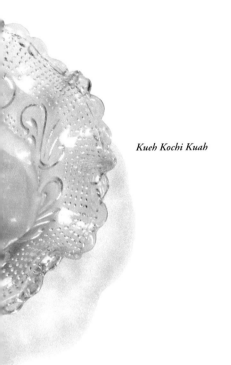

Kueh Kochi Kuah

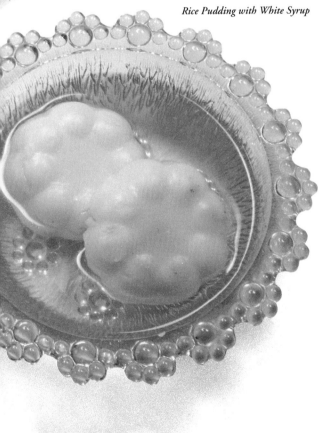

Rice Pudding with White Syrup

KUEH KOCHI KUAH

Ingredients for the filling:
- [ ] *1 cup grated coconut - with or without skin*
- [ ] *1 cup brown sugar*
- [ ] *$^1/_4$ cup water*

Ingredients for glutinous rice dough:
- [ ] *$1^1/_2$ cups glutinous rice flour* (tepong pulot)
- [ ] *$^1/_4$ tsp green food colouring*
- [ ] *1 tsp salt*
- [ ] *$^1/_2$ cup water*
- [ ] *2 fragrant screwpine leaves - pound and extract juice*

Ingredients for sauce
- [ ] *230g grated coconut - without skin add 2 cups water and extract 2 cups coconut milk*
- [ ] *2 level tbsp plain or rice flour*
- [ ] *2 fragrant screwpine leaves* (daun pandan)

Method for filling:

Combine ingredients and cook over low heat till thick, stirring all the time. Set aside to cool then shape into little balls, the size of small marbles.

Method for rice dough:

Put the glutinous rice flour in a bowl. Add colouring, juice of pandan leaves, salt and enough water from the half cup allowance to form a dough. Take a small lump of dough, flatten, put a ball of filling in the middle and wrap dough round it, shaping it into a ball. In a saucepan, heat water to which a little salt and one pandan leaf has been added. When water is boiling, drop in the balls of dough. When they rise to the surface, they are cooked. Remove, drain and put them in the sauce.

Method for sauce:

Combine all the ingredients and bring to the boil, stirring all the time. When fairly thick, remove from heat. Cool a little.

UBI CERAH
(Tapioca Chips Coated in Gula Melaka)

Ingredients:
- [ ] 600g fresh tapioca - peel, wash and slice very thin
- [ ] 1 block palm sugar (gula Melaka) - cut into pieces
- [ ] 5 tbsp water
- [ ] oil for deep frying

Method:
Rub tapioca slices with salt then deep fry till light brown; drain and cool.

Put gula Melaka and water in a pan and dissolve over low heat, then add the tapioca slices and stir till they are well coated with syrup. Remove from heat. Leave to cool before storing in an air tight container.

RICE PUDDING WITH WHITE SYRUP

Ingredients:
- [ ] 1 cup rice flour
- [ ] 450g grated coconut - add 2 cups water and extract 4 cups milk
- [ ] 1 level tbsp tapioca flour
- [ ] 1 tsp salt
- [ ] 2-3 fragrant screwpine leaves (daun pandan)

Method:
Combine rice flour, coconut milk, tapioca flour and salt. Stir and strain into a saucepan.

Add pandan leaves and cook, stirring all the time.

When thick, remove from heat, put into individual moulds or into a tray and chill.

When serving, pour syrup over pudding.

Syrup Ingredients:
- [ ] 1 cup granulated sugar
- [ ] 2 cups water
- [ ] 1 fragrant screwpine leaf (daun pandan)

Method:
Combine the above ingredients in a saucepan and bring to the boil.

Cool before pouring over pudding.

SERIKAYA BERAS
(Steamed Rice-Custard Cake)

Ingredients:
- [ ] 5 eggs
- [ ] 230g sugar
- [ ] 450g grated coconut - without adding water, squeeze coconut to obtain 1 cup thick milk
- [ ] 2 slightly heaped tbsp rice flour
- [ ] 3-4 fragrant screwpine leaves (daun pandan)
- [ ] pinch of salt
- [ ] 2 drops green food colouring
- [ ] pinch of vanillin crystals, or drop of vanilla essence (optiona

Method:
Boil water in steamer.

Beat eggs and sugar in a bowl till sugar dissolves, then add coconut milk and stir. Add rice flour, stir, add juice of pandan leaves, salt, colouring and vanilla. Mix well and strai mixture into a sandwich tin. Steam for 10 minutes then stir. Cover and steam for another 20 minutes.

Allow to cool before cutting.

ONDEH ONDEH KELEDE
(Sweet Potato Balls)

Ingredients:
- [ ] 600g sweet potatoes - boil in water to which 2 fragrant screwpine leaves (daun pandan) have been added, peel then mash while still warm.
- [ ] 4 fragrant screwpine leaves (daun pandan) - pound to extract juice
- [ ] 4 heaped tbsp plain flour
- [ ] 1 block palm sugar (gula Melaka) - cut into little slivers
- [ ] 230g grated coconut - (remove skin) steam with a little salt to prevent the coconut from going sour

Method:
Squeeze juice from crushed pandan leaves into mashed sweet potatoes. Add flour and a pinch of salt and mix. Take a small lump of dough, flatten it, put a few slivers of gula Melaka in the middle and roll into a ball. Repeat till all the dough is used up.

Boil a pan of water. Drop sweet potato balls into boiling water.

Remove when they rise to the surface, drain and roll in steamed coconut.

RICE DOUGH

If rice dough is not available at the market, it can be easily made with the use of a liquidiser or blender.

To get the dough really fine and smooth may take a bit of time, causing the liquidiser to get heated. It is therefore suggested that after every 5 minutes, the liquidiser should be switched off to allow it to cool for a couple of minutes.

Ingredients:
- [ ] *600g broken rice* (**beras hancor**) *- clean, wash and soak 4 to 5 hours or preferably overnight*
- [ ] *2 cups water*

Method:
Strain rice. Put half the amount of rice and water in liquidiser. Liquidise till very fine; repeat with rest of rice and water.

KUEH JONGKONG

Ingredients:
- [ ] *2 cups rice flour*
- [ ] *2 level tbsp tapioca flour*
- [ ] *680g grated coconut - add 4 cups water and extract 6 cups milk*
- [ ] *1 fragrant screwpine leaf (daun pandan)*
- [ ] *1 tsp salt*
- [ ] *1 cylindrical block palm sugar* (**gula Melaka**) *- cut into little slivers*

Method:
Combine rice flour, tapioca flour, coconut milk and salt. Mix and strain into a saucepan.

Break pandan leaf into mixture then cook over low heat, stirring all the time. When the mixture becomes fairly thick, remove from heat.

To wrap into bundles:
Have ready about 12 to 15 pieces of banana leaves each measuring 25cm x 15cm (10 x 6in).

Put two tablespoons of cooked mixture on banana leaf. Put a heaped teaspoon of gula Melaka in the centre of the mixture, put another tablespoon of mixture over this and fold bundle in this way:

bring the two lengths of the leaf towards the centre so that they overlap, covering the mixture; tuck the two ends underneath.

Put bundles in steamer (boil water in steamer beforehand) and steam for 20 minutes. Serve cold.

KUEH LAPIS BERAS

Ingredients:
- [ ] *450g sugar*
- [ ] *2 cups water (for boiling sugar)*
- [ ] *2 fragrant screwpine leaves* (**daun pandan**)
- [ ] *900g grated coconut (remove skin) - for* first squeeze, *add 1 cup water; using a fine tea towel or piece of muslin, extract 2 cups thick milk. For* second squeeze, *add 1 cup water to coconut and extract equal amount of milk.*
- [ ] *600g rice dough*
- [ ] *4 heaped tbsp tapioca flour*
- [ ] *pinch of salt*
- [ ] *$^1/_2$ tsp cochineal*

Points to note:
When making nonya kueh such as Kueh Lapis Beras, to obtain thick, rich milk from coconut, use either a fine tea towel or a piece of muslin to squeeze coconut.

Use a fine mesh strainer to strain mixture before steaming. If rice flour is used instead of rice dough, the kueh will not be fine in texture.

Make sure that each layer is firm before adding the next. When one layer is opaque or milky looking, not transparent, then add the next layer, pouring the mixture in gently.

Method:
Boil water in steamer.

Put sugar, water and pandan leaves in a saucepan and heat till sugar dissolves.

Leave syrup until it is luke warm, then add to coconut milk (first squeeze). Combine rice dough with tapioca flour and salt. Add coconut milk (second squeeze) and mix to a smooth paste, then add coconut milk-syrup. Stir till smooth and well mixed then strain with fine mesh strainer. Grease a square or round (27cm or 11 in diameter) sandwich tin. Heat tin in steamer for about 5 minutes.

Put 4 cups of mixture in a bowl and colour with cochineal. Leave the rest of the mixture white. Pour 1 cup of white mixture into the heated tray and steam for 6-8 minutes, then add $^3/_4$ cup red mixture over first layer, pouring it gently. Steam for 5 minutes.

Repeat process, steaming white and red layers alternately till all the mixture is used up. For the last layer, which should be red, pour 1 cup mixture and steam for 10-12 minutes.

Cut when thoroughly cool.

Note: If desired, 3 different colours may be used.

Pulut Serikaya

Kueh Keswi

Kueh Lompang

Kueh Jongkong

Kueh Lapis Beras

KUEH KESWI

Ingredients:

- [ ] *150g palm sugar* (gula Melaka)
- [ ] *75g brown sugar*
- [ ] *75g granulated sugar*
- [ ] *200ml water (for boiling sugar)*
- [ ] *1 fragrant screwpine leaf* (daun pandan)
- [ ] *300g rice dough (see Rice Dough recipe)*
- [ ] *2¹/₂ heaped tbsp tapioca flour*
- [ ] *¹/₄ tsp lime (kapor) [see glossary] - mix with a little*
  water into paste
- [ ] *¹/₄ tsp salt*
- [ ] *250ml water*
- [ ] *120g grated coconut (remove skin)* ⎫
- [ ] *1 tsp salt* ⎭ *mix*

Method:

Boil water in steamer.

Put all the sugar, water and pandan leaf in a saucepan and heat until sugar dissolves, stirring occasionally. Strain and cool.

Put rice dough, tapioca flour, kapor, salt and water in a large bowl and mix to a smooth consistency.

Add to luke warm syrup, stir well then strain. Fill either individual small moulds or deep trays with mixture. (Small Chinese teacups can be used as moulds; they should be heated in steamer for about 2 - 3 minutes before using).

Steam kueh for not more than 20 minutes. When cooked, stand moulds in a shallow tray of cold water. When cold, remove kueh from moulds by loosening edge with a knife.

Serve with grated coconut which has been mixed with salt.

Makes about 35 to 37.

PULOT SERIKAYA

Ingredients for first layer:
- ☐ **600g glutinous rice (beras pulot)** - *wash and soak overnight in water to which a little salt has been added*
- ☐ **1.35kg grated coconut** - *without skin. Extract 2 cups thick milk without adding water and reserve this for 2nd layer; then add 1 cup water to coconut and extract 1 cup milk for lst layer*
- ☐ **1 fragrant screwpine leaf (daun pandan)**
- ☐ **salt**

Ingredients for second layer:
- ☐ **300g sugar**
- ☐ **5 eggs**
- ☐ **4 fragrant screwpine leaves (daun pandan)** - *cut into small pieces and pound to extract juice*
- ☐ **1 tsp green food colouring**
- ☐ **$1/_4$ tsp vanillin crystals, or vanilla essence (optional)**
- ☐ **3 level tbsp plain flour** - *sieve*
- ☐ **2 cups thick coconut milk**

Method for first layer:
Boil water in steamer.

Drain rice and put in steaming tray or sandwich tin, approx. 25cm (10in) diameter for a round tray or 20cm (8in) square for a square tray.

Add coconut milk, pinch of salt, pandan leaf broken into two. Stir then steam. After 20 minutes, turn rice over with a fork and continue steaming. After another 10 minutes, take tray out and press rice down with a piece of folded banana leaf till flat and compact. Steam for 5 more minutes.

Method for second layer:
Combine sugar and eggs in a fairly large bowl, and beat till sugar dissolves. Add flour, colouring, vanillin, juice from pandan leaf and mix well, then add coconut milk, stir and strain mixture.

To combine first and second layers:
When the first layer is cooked, prick the rice all over with a fork to ensure that the second layer adheres to it.

Pour the mixture for the second layer slowly over the first and steam for 10 minutes.

Remove lid, gently stir the top layer which is beginning to solidify, mixing it with the liquid, then continue steaming for 30 minutes.

When top layer is firm, remove and allow to cool well before cutting.

KUEH LOMPANG

Ingredients:
- ☐ **225g granulated sugar**
- ☐ **250ml water (for boiling sugar)**
- ☐ **1 fragrant screwpine leaf (daun pandan)**
- ☐ **300g rice dough** (*see Rice Dough recipe*)
- ☐ **$2^1/_2$ level tbsp tapioca flour**
- ☐ **250ml (1 cup) water**
- ☐ **$1/_4$ tsp salt**
- ☐ **food colouring** - *3 to 4 colours*
- ☐ **120g grated coconut (remove skin)** ⎫
- ☐ **1 tsp salt** ⎬ mix

Method:
Boil water in steamer.

Put pandan leaf, sugar and water in a pot and heat until sugar dissolves. Strain and cool.

Put rice dough, tapioca flour, salt and water in a large bowl and mix to a smooth consistency.

Pour luke warm syrup into rice mixture and stir well, then strain. Put mixture in 3 or 4 bowls of the same size (depending on the number of colours you plan to use). Add a drop or two of colouring to each bowl of mixture and stir well. Pour mixture into little Chinese teacups (one size smaller then those used for kueh keswi) which have been pre-heated in steamer and steam for not more than 20 minutes.

Repeat steaming process till all the mixture has been used, making sure each time that the teacups are heated in steamer before mixture is poured into them.

When cooked, stand moulds in a shallow tray of cold water; when cold, remove kueh from moulds by loosening edge with a knife.

Serve with grated coconut which has been mixed with salt.

Makes about 45 to 50.

GULAB JAMUN
(Milk Sweets in Syrup)

Ingredients:
- [ ] 4 cups milk powder
- [ ] 1 cup self-raising flour
- [ ] 4 tbsp ghee
- [ ] 250ml (1 cup) fresh milk
- [ ] ghee for deep frying

Ingredients for syrup:
- [ ] 3 cups sugar
- [ ] 3 cups water
- [ ] 1 stick cinnamon 3cm ($1\frac{1}{4}$ in) long
- [ ] 5 cloves
- [ ] 5 cardamoms

Method:
Combine all ingredients (except ghee for frying) in a bowl. Make little balls the size of walnuts.

Heat ghee then fry milk balls over low heat till dark brown. Drain, cool a little, then put milk balls into syrup.

Serve when cold.

Method for syrup:
Put all ingredients in a saucepan and boil till sugar dissolves.

Remove and cool a little before putting in the milk balls.

Sevian or Semiah

Gulab Jamun

Gajjah Ki Halwa

Badam Halwa

BADAM HALWA
(Almond Sweet)

Ingredients:
- [ ] 230g sugar
- [ ] 6 tbsp water
- [ ] 180g ground almonds
- [ ] 180g butter or ghee
- [ ] 2 tsp rose water
- [ ] 6 cardamoms - *remove seeds from pod and crush them*
- [ ] pinch of salt

Method:
Dissolve sugar in water over low heat, then bring to the boil.

Add almonds, rose water, butter or ghee and salt, then keep stirring.

When mixture thickens, pour into a shallow dish and sprinkle the crushed cardamom seeds on top.

Leave to cool before cutting into squares or diamond shapes.

Decorate with cherries.

SEVIAN OR SEMIAH

Ingredients:
- [ ] 6 tbsp ghee
- [ ] 120g cashew nuts
- [ ] 120g sultanas
- [ ] 150g yellow vermicelli - break into 3 pieces
- [ ] $1\frac{1}{4}$ litre fresh milk (5 cups)
- [ ] 230g granulated sugar
- [ ] 1 tbsp rose water

Method:
Heat ghee in large, heavy saucepan. Deep fry cashew nuts then the sultanas separately. Drain and keep aside.

Fry vermicelli in remaining ghee till brown, then add milk. Keep stirring, add sugar and rose water. Bring to the boil then continue to boil for a few more minutes. Add sultanas and cashew nuts, cover, reduce heat and cook till vermicelli is soft. Serve hot.

GAJJAH KI HALWA

Ingredients:
- [ ] *600g carrots - peel and grate coarsely*
- [ ] *750ml (3 cups) fresh milk*
- [ ] *450g granulated sugar*
- [ ] *2 tsp rose water*
- [ ] *3 tbsp ghee*
- [ ] *60g almonds - scald, remove skin and chop*
- [ ] *120g sultanas*
- [ ] *120g cashew nuts - cut each in half and fry in 2 tbsp ghee till golden brown*
- [ ] *10 cardamoms - slit pods, remove seeds and discard pods*

Method:
Put grated carrots and milk in a large, heavy saucepan and cook over high heat.

When liquid is reduced by half, add sugar, ghee and rose water, and continue cooking stirring now and then. When sugar has dissolved, lower heat, add almonds and cook for about 5 minutes. Add sultanas and continue to cook, stirring frequently.

When almost dry, add cashew nuts. When the mixture is dry and leaves the sides of the pan, remove from heat and sprinkle with cardamom seeds.

Spread mixture in a sandwich tin or cake tray and allow to cool, then cut into square or diamond shapes.

Alternatively, put a tablespoonful of mixture in the centre of a rectangular piece of cellophane paper, decorate with a cherry and almond slivers and wrap into a neat package. Repeat till all the mixture is used.

Note: The whole cooking process takes about an hour.

URAP PISANG
(Sliced Banana in Grated Coconut)

Ingredients:
- [ ] *12 ripe pisang kepok or pisang nipah - wash unpeeled, and steam for 15 minutes*
- [ ] *230g grated coconut - remove skin before grating*
- [ ] *2 tbsp sugar*
- [ ] *$^1/_2$ tsp salt*

Method:
Peel steamed bananas and cut into thick slices. Mix coconut with sugar and salt, add banana slices and mix.

Chocolate Sponge Pudding

Orange Jelly

Penggat Pisang

Urap Pisang

Magic Jelly

115

PENGGAT PISANG
(Banana in Gula Melaka Syrup)

Ingredients:
- [ ] 300g palm sugar (gula Melaka)
- [ ] 1 1/2 cups water
- [ ] 2 1/2 tbsp granulated sugar
- [ ] 5 ripe bananas (pisang kepok) - cut each in two, lengthwise
- [ ] 1 fragrant screwpine leaf (daun pandan) - wash and tie
- [ ] 1 small bundle bean thread vermicelli (sohoon) - soak for a few minutes then cut into shorter lengths (optional)

Coconut Milk Sauce:
Mix 230g grated coconut (remove skin) with 1/2 cup boiled water and extract the thick coconut milk, then add a pinch of salt.

Method:
Combine gula Melaka, granulated sugar, water and pandan leaf in a saucepan and put over heat to dissolve sugar.

When sugar has dissolved, strain syrup into another saucepan, add bananas and sohoon (if used). Bring to the boil and leave to cook for 5 minutes.

Serve with Coconut Milk Sauce.

ORANGE JELLY

Ingredients:
- [ ] 1/2 packet (15g) agar-agar strands - soak for 1/2 an hour
- [ ] 4 cups water
- [ ] 1/2 can evaporated milk (410g / 369ml)
- [ ] 1 egg
- [ ] 225g granulated sugar
- [ ] 1 tsp orange essence
- [ ] 1/2 tsp yellow food colouring

Method:
Boil agar-agar in water. When dissolved, strain into another saucepan. Mix the milk with egg, half the amount of sugar and essence in a large bowl. Dissolve the rest of the sugar in a large saucepan and cook till sugar becomes brown and cystallizes.

Combine milk mixture with jelly and add to crystallized sugar. Cook, stirring all the time, until it boils, then continue cooking for a minute or two. Remove from heat and pour into large jelly moulds or trays. Leave to cool, then chill in fridge.

CHOCOLATE SPONGE PUDDING

Ingredients:
- [ ] 290g butter or margarine
- [ ] 290g caster sugar
- [ ] 6 eggs
- [ ] 290g plain flour ⎫
- [ ] 2 tsp baking powder ⎬ mix
- [ ] 2 tbsp cocoa
- [ ] 3-4 tbsp warm water

Ingredients for custard sauce:
- [ ] 1 egg
- [ ] 1 tbsp sugar
- [ ] 250ml (1 cup) milk
- [ ] 2 tsp custard powder - add 2 tbsp milk from allowance and mix well

Method:
Cream butter and sugar until light and fluffy. Beat in eggs, one at a time.

Fold in the sieved flour and cocoa, adding sufficient water to make a soft dropping consistency so that mixture drops readily from spoon.

Pour mixture into a greased pudding basin, filling it only three-quarters full to allow room for pudding to rise.

Steam for 1-1 1/4 hrs.

Turn out on a dish. If it appears to stick, loosen edges with a blunt knife. Serve at once with custard sauce.

Method for custard sauce:
Beat egg and sugar lightly in a saucepan. Add rest of milk and heat. When almost boiling, gradually add custard powder stirring all the time. Cook over low heat till mixture boils and thickens.

MAGIC JELLY

Ingredients:
- [ ] *1 packet agar-agar strands*
- [ ] *450g granulated sugar*
- [ ] *200ml fresh milk*
- [ ] *2 fragrant screwpine leaves* (**daun pandan**) *- wash and tie into a knot*
- [ ] *6 cups water*
- [ ] *1 tsp rose essence*
- [ ] *yellow, green, red and blue food colouring*

Method:

Soak agar-agar for 1 hour then drain.

Put agar-agar, pandan leaves and water in a large pot. Bring to the boil, then continue boiling till agar-agar dissolves. Add sugar, stir and when sugar dissolves, strain jelly into a large bowl. Add milk and essence to jelly and stir. Put 2 large ladles of jelly in each of four small shallow bowls, leaving rest in large bowl. Add a different colour to each small bowl and chill coloured jelly in fridge. Leave the white mixture at room temperature to prevent it setting before coloured jellies. When the bowls of coloured jelly have set, cut them into small cubes, add to the white mixture and stir to mix. Pour into jelly moulds and chill.

FRESH & DRIED NOODLES

Flat or Ribbon Rice Noodles
(Kwei Teow)

Fresh Yellow Noodles
(Mee)

Dried Rice Vermicelli
(Beehoon)

Fresh Rice Noodles
(Laksa Beehoon)

Macaroni

Dried Rice Noodles
(Beehoon Kasar)

BEANCURD

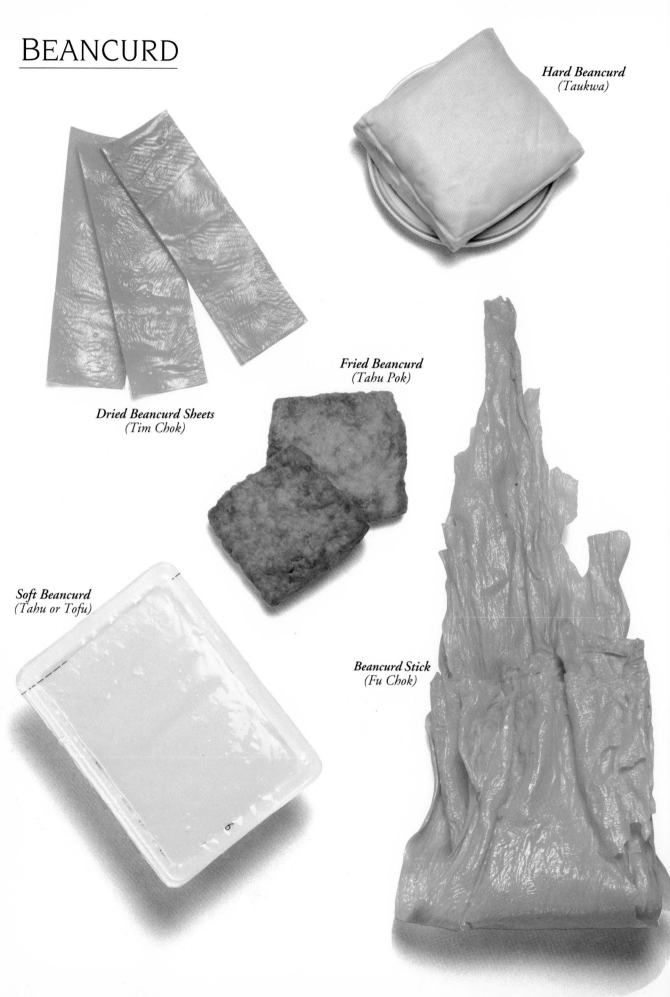

Hard Beancurd
(Taukwa)

Dried Beancurd Sheets
(Tim Chok)

Fried Beancurd
(Tahu Pok)

Soft Beancurd
(Tahu or Tofu)

Beancurd Stick
(Fu Chok)

DRIED/SALTED

Black Fungus
Soaked in Water

Black Fungus
(Telinga Tikus)

Dried Lily Buds
(Kim Chiam)

Salted Ikan Kurau

Maldive Fish

Dried Anchovies
(Dried Ikan Bilis)

Dried Shrimps
(Udang Kering)

Dried Silver Fish

ROOTS AND LEAVES

Sweet Potato Leaf
(Daun Keledek)

Tapioca
(Ubi)

Sweet Potato
(Keledek)

Yam
(Keladi)

ROOTS AND LEAVES

Fragrant Lime Leaves
(Daun Limau Purut)

Curry Leaves
(Daun Kari)

Spring Onion

Daun Kesom
(Bol: polygonum)

Chekor Leaves

Chekor Root
(Fragrant Ginger Root)

Mint *(Daun Pudina)*

Coriander Leaves
(Duan Ketumbar Kasar)

Fragrant Screwpine
(Daun Pandan)

Lemon Grass
(Serai)

Bunga Siantan
(Red Ginger Plant Bud)

Turmeric Leaf
(Daun Kunyit)

Fresh Ginger Root
(old)

Fresh Ginger Root
(young)

Galangal Root
(Lengkuas)

Fresh Turmeric Root
(Kunyit Basah)

FISH *(Fresh)*

White Pomfret
(Ikan Bawal Putih)

Black Pomfret
(Ikan Bawal Hitam)

Sting Ray
(Ikan Pari Nyiru)

Shark
(Ikan Yu)

Tunny
(Ikan Tongkol)

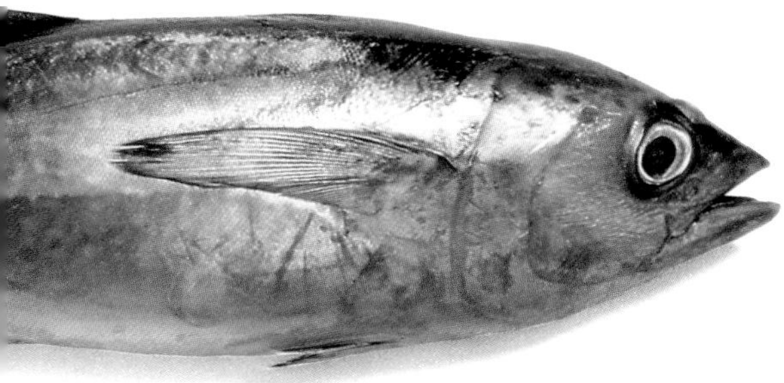

Ikan Kledek

Tilapia

Horse Mackerel
(Ikan Selah)

Sea Bass

FISH *(Fresh)*

Ikan Kerisi
(Sea Bream)

Ikan Kurau Head
(Threadfin)

Ikan Parang
(Wolf Herring)

Ikan Kambong
(Chubb Mackerel)

Ikan Kuning
(Yellow Banded Scad)

129

FISH & CRUSTACEANS *(Fresh)*

Kepah
(Small Clams)

Ikan Cencaru
(Torpedo Fish)

Ikan Tenggiri
(Spanish Mackerel)

Ikan Tamban
(Round Herring)

Squid
(Sotong)

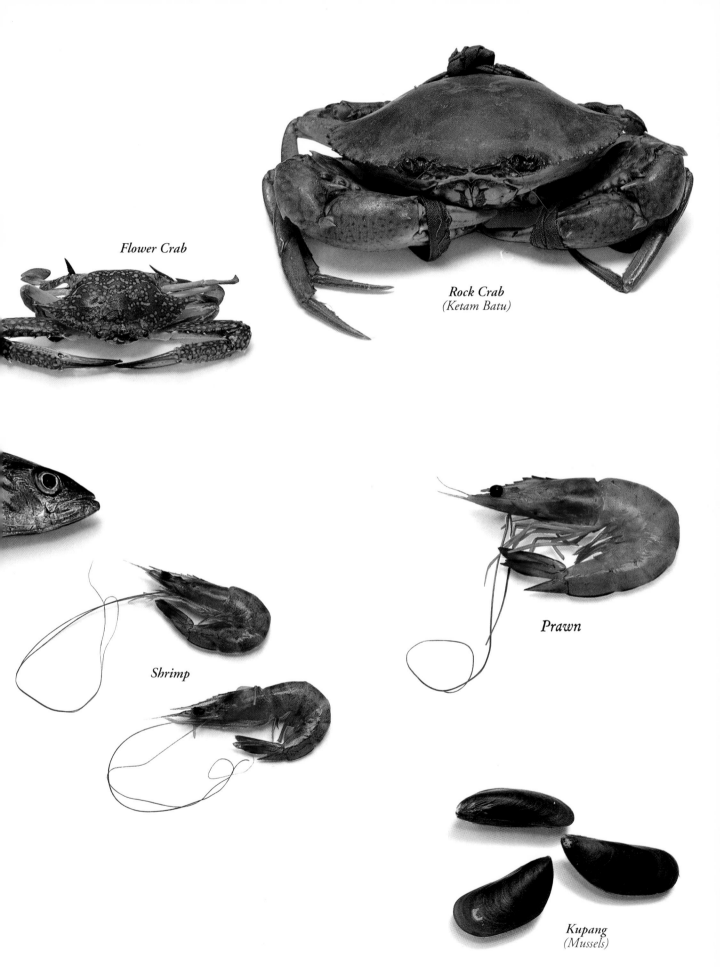

Flower Crab

Rock Crab
(Ketam Batu)

Prawn

Shrimp

Kupang
(Mussels)

SPICES

Cloves
(Bunga Chengkeh)

Black Peppercorn

Fennel
(Jintan Manis)

COMPOUNDED ASAFOETIDA ®

Asafoetida
(Hing)

Cumin
(Jintan Puteh)

Fish Curry Spices
or Whole Seed Spices
(Rempah Tumis Ikan)

Dark Fine Cumin
(Sajira)

Cinnamon Bark
(Kayu Manis)

Coriander
(Ketumbar)

Saffron Strands
(Koma-Koma)

Mustard Seeds
(Biji Sawi)

Cardamom
(Buah Pelaga)

Fenugreek
(Alba)

Dried Turmeric Roots
(Kunyit Kering)

VEGETABLES & FRUIT

Pisang Rajah

Pisang Kepok

Brinjal *(Long green and purple ones usually used in Chinese cookery. Round purple ones used in curries.)*

*Water Convolvulus
(Kangkong)*

*Unripe Jackfruit
(Nangka)*

Chinese Celery

*Fragrant Lime
(Limau Purut)*

Pisang Kari

Green, unripe Mango

Blimbing

Pumpkin
(*Labu Merah*)

Yam Bean
(*Bangkwang*)

*Fresh Red
and Green Chilli*

Snake Gourd

Birds-Eye Chilli
(*Chilli Padi*)

Small Limes
(*Limau Kesturi*)

Bitter Gourd

Hairy Gourd

Long or String Beans

Ladies Fingers

Chinese Radish
(*Lobak Puteh*)

Drumstick

DRIED FOODSTUFF

Chick Peas
(Kacang Kuda)

Sesame Seeds
(Bijian)

Green Beans
(Kacang Hijau)

Black Gram
with skin removed

Wheat Grains
(Terigu)

Black Gram
(Ulundu)

Lentils

Basmati Rice

Broken Rice

Fine Wholemeal Flour
(Ata Flour)

Oil Chilli

Cashew Nuts

Dried Mata Kuching
(Dried Longans)

Crinkly Chilli

Dried Chillies

Candlenut
(Buah Keras)

Kamang Semangkok

Katira

Bean Thread Vermicelli
(Sohoon)

Almond

Biji Selaseh

Nutmeg
(Buah Pala)

Dried Tamarind Slice
(Asam Keping or Asam Gelugor)

Quail Eggs

Blacan
(Dried Shrimp Paste)

Pink Blacan
(For Cooking)

Dark Blacan
(For Sambal Blacan)

137

UTENSILS

Griddle or Hot Plate
(Tawa)

Steamer
(2-tiered)

Pestle and Mortar
(Batu Lesong)

Idli Steamer with 2 trays

Grater

Egg Poacher
*(may be used as substitute for
Idli Steamer)*

North Indian Spice Container
for Whole Seed Spices
and Spice Powders

Set of Aluminium Curry Pots

Inverted Bamboo Colander
on which Putu Mayam
is placed for steaming

Metric Cup

2.5 ml approx ¹/₂ tsp

5 ml approx. 1 tsp

Set of Metric Spoons

Winding Dough Press
(for making Putu Mayam
and Murukku)

10 ml approx. 1 dessert tsp

15 ml approx. 1 tbsp

Glossary

AGAR AGAR: a type of gelatine made from seaweed that sets without refrigeration. Available in strands, which must be soaked in water for $1/2$ hour before use, or powder. Strands are used in this book, but powder agar agar can be substituted (1 teaspoon will set approximately 2 cups water). If using powder, pre-soaking is unnecessary. Ordinary gelatine cannot be used as a substitute.

ASAFOETIDA: a gum derived from a Persian plant that is used in tiny amounts in Indian cooking to give flavour and to prevent flatulence. Available in small rectangular blocks from Indian spice shops; known as *hing* in Hindi and *perankayam* in Tamil.

ASAM: see Tamarind

BANANAS: In savoury dishes, non-sweet bananas similar to plantains are used (such as *pisang kepok, pisang kari, pisang nipah*). Be sure not to substitute with sweet dessert bananas. Banana leaf is frequently used to wrap cakes and fish. Foil can be substituted in most cases, although the flavour will be different.

BASMATI: fragrant long-grain rice usually from Pakistan, it has a delicious nutty flavour. Sometimes sold as *Patna* rice. Available in Indian shops and in some health food shops.

BEAN CURD: the soya bean is one of the most versatile products in Asia. Bean curd made from soya beans is available in several consistencies. The firm bean curd is known as *taukwa*, and is available in local market, supermarket or Chinese delicatessens overseas. Do not confuse with soft beancurd (*tahu*). Dried bean curd skin, available in sticks (*fu chok*) or sheets (*tim chok*) is sold loose or in packages.

BEAN THREAD VERMICELLI: called *sohoon*, or sometimes *tunghoon*, locally these fine transparent noodles are also known as *fun see*. They are made from flour of the dried green *mung* bean.

BESAN: flour made from chick peas (*kacang kuda*). Sometimes called 'gram flour'. Do not confuse with flour made from yellow lentils.

BLIMBING: a small oblong acidic fruit used by Malay and some Chinese cooks. Green tomatoes could be used as a substitute.

BRIANI SPICES: ready-mixed spices for use in Nasi Briani sold by some Indian spice merchants, consisting of cinnamon, cloves, cardamom, and a spice known as 'black cumin' (sajira) which is thinner than regular cumin and has a different flavour.

BROWN MUSTARD SEEDS: small seeds used by South Indian cooks, known as *biji sawi*. Do not confuse with the larger yellow mustard seeds from Europe - the flavour is quite different.

CANDLENUTS: a cream-coloured waxy nut (*buah keras*) used for texture in Malay and Indonesian dishes. Substitute macadamia nuts or cashews.

CHICK PEA FLOUR: see Besan

CHILLIES: unless otherwise specified in recipe, use fresh chillies of the variety that is about 10-15cm (4-6in) long. Birds-eye chill (*chilli padi*) are about 2cm($3/4$in) long and very hot. *Chill-tairu* are green chillies preserved in salted yoghurt; store in tins and deep fry in hot oil for a few seconds.

COARSE CHIVES: Flat dark green chives known as *kuchai*, available in markets or Chinese delicatessens overseas. Slightly different flavour to fine round chives; the green tops of spring onions would be an acceptable substitute.

COCONUTS: Freshly grated coconut is used to make coconut milk by adding water and squeezing to obtain the liquid. If you cannot obtain fresh coconuts the following methods can be used to obtain coconut milk:

Creamed Coconut: a solid preparation sold in round plastic tubs. To obtain thick coconut milk, mix 100g ($3^1/2$ oz) creamed coconut with 1 cup boiling water. Stir until dissolved and strain while still hot. For thin coconut milk, use 30g(1 oz) creamed coconut to 1 cup water.

Desiccated Coconut: blend 2 cups desiccated coconut with 2 cups water in a blender. Mix at high speed for 30 seconds, then squeeze and strain for thick coconut milk. Return coconut to blender and mix with another 2½ cups hot water and repeat the process to obtain thin coconut milk.

Cakes can be made using desiccated coconut moistened with a little milk if fresh coconuts are not available, although naturally the flavour is not quite as good.

CORIANDER LEAVES: known as *wan swee* to Chinese cooks, these leaves have a distinctive flavour. The 'small' coriander leaves specified in some recipes are actually the first leaves of the young coriander seedling, and are milder in flavour than the mature leaves. The Malay name for 'small' coriander is *daun ketumbar halus*; if the leaves are not available, use the 'big' leaves, *daun ketumbar kasar*. If you have difficulty obtaining fresh coriander leaves, try growing them in a pot from the coriander spice seeds that you buy in a spice shop.

CURRY LEAVES: used abundantly by South Indian cooks, curry leaves (*karuvapillai* in Tamil, *daun kari* in Malay) must not be confused with the Indonesian *daun salam*, a type of bay leaf. Curry leaves are about 2.5cm (1 in) long, dark green in colour, and have a pungent smell. Dried leaves can be bought overseas in specialist curry shops.

DAUN KESOM: a pungent dark green herb (bot:polygonum); nearest substitute is mint.

DRIED GREEN BEAN: this is the *mung* bean, a tiny green pea-shaped bean known as *lok tau* by Chinese cooks, and *kacang hijau* by Malays. Flour made from this bean is known as *tepong hoen kwe*.

DRIED LILY BUDS: sometimes called 'golden needles,' a direct translation of the Chinese name *kim chiam*, these are slender golden-brown strips about 8cm (3in) long.

DRIED SHRIMP PASTE: called *blacan* by Malays, trassi by Indonesians, this is a very strong-smelling seasoning which gives an authentic touch to many dishes.

DRIED ANCHOVIES: these range in size from the very tiny thin variety often known as 'silver fish' up to the large variety about 5cm (2in) long. If using large ones, discard head. Known as *ikan bilis*, these fish have been salted before being dried, so always taste a recipe using these before adding salt.

EGGPLANT: Malay name is terong, the Indian name is *brinjal*. Asian varieties are much smaller than European eggplant or aubergine, and are generally around 15-18cm (6-7in) in length.

FISH CURRY SPICES: also known as *rempah tumis ikan*, this is a mixture of whole spices including brown mustard seed, fenugreek, cumin, fennel and husked blackgram dhal (*biji sawi, alba, jintan puteh, jintan manis and urad dhal*). If you cannot obtain this ready-mixed from your spice shop, mix your own using 1 teaspoon of each spice except for fenugreek, which should be just ½ teaspoon.

FRAGRANT LIME LEAVES: a wonderfully fragrant leaf from a variety of citrus, known as *daun limau purut*. Any young citrus leaves could be substituted, although their flavour is nowhere near as lovely.

FRAGRANT SCREWPINE LEAF: a variety of *pandanus* palm known as *daun pandan* and used to flavour cakes and desserts. It is a long (at least 30cm or 12in), narrow, shiny leaf, easily grown in a tropical garden.

FRESH RICE FLOUR NOODLES: sometimes sold in a wide flat sheet which you must cut into strips with scissors, otherwise sold ready-cut. Known as *kwei teow* or *sa hor fun*. Available dried from Chinese stores overseas; if using the dried noodles, soak in boiling water for ½ hour, drain, and soak in a second lot of boiling water for another ½ hour.

FRIED SHALLOTS: used for garnishing. Finely slice fresh shallots and deep fry till golden brown. Drain and store in air tight bottle. Keep in refrigerator. Use as garnishing for soup etc.

GHEE: butter oil favoured by Indian cooks since it does not burn as readily as butter. Obtainable in tins from Indian stores. To make your own *ghee*, heat a packet of butter over very low heat until it melts. Allow sediment to sink to the bottom of the pan, then pour off the golden oil sitting on the top. Put oil into a clean saucepan, heat again, then strain through muslin to remove any trace of sediment. Keeps several months without refrigeration.

GLUTINOUS RICE: a variety of rice which becomes very sticky when cooked; used mostly for cakes and known as *pulot*. Generally available in Chinese stores.

KAPOR: white lime used as part of a *betel* quid. Obtainable in Asia from Indian *betel* sellers; elsewhere, try chemist shops.

LEMON GRASS: a type of grass with a pungent lemony

fragrance, this is used to make citronella. Known as *serai*, it grows like a small leek bulb. Use only the bottom 10-15cm (4-6in), discarding the tough upper leaves. Strips of dried lemon grass are sometimes sold under the Indonesian name *sereh*. Powdered *serai* or *sereh* can also be substituted; use about 1 teaspoon in place of 1 stalk of fresh lemon grass.

LENGKUAS: a ginger-like root of the galangal family, this is known locally only by its Malay name *lengkuas*. Powdered *lengkuas* or *laos* (the Indonesian name) is often obtainable in curry shops overseas; substitute 1 teaspoon of powder for 1 thick slice of fresh *lengkuas*.

LIMES: two types of limes can be used; the large green lime, which is shaped like a lemon, and the small round lime, which is known as *limau kesturi*. The small lime has more fragrance than the large variety; substitute half-ripe kumquats if possible, otherwise use lemon juice.

LOCAL VINEGAR: very strong synthetic vinegar used by many Singapore cooks. If using regular white vinegar such as Heinz, use only half the amount specified for local vinegar.

OMUM: a minute spice resembling parsley seed, this is used to flavour Murukku and some other Indian dishes. The botanical name is *carom*, the Hindi *ajwain*. No substitute.

PALM SUGAR: known as *gula Melaka*, this is a hard brown sugar made from the sap of the *aren* palm. If not available, substitute soft brown sugar with a touch of maple syrup. Often sold in cylindrical blocks.

PAPADUM: also spelled *popadum*, these are paper-thin wafers made from lentil flour. They should be absolutely dry before frying in hot oil for a few seconds on either side, so that they swell up and become crisp and golden.

RICE VERMICELLI: popularly called *beehoon*, this noodle is a very thin white thread made from rice flour. Sometimes called *mi fun* or rice stick noodles.

ROSE WATER: a wonderfully evocative flavour, this is Arabian in origin. Used in some Indian and Malay dishes. If using the concentrated rose essence, be sure to use much less than the amount required for rose water, which is diluted.

SALTED SOYA BEANS: soft brown salty beans in a thick paste, called *taucheo*. Sometimes sold in jars labelled 'bean sauce' in Western countries.

SAJIRA: dark fine cumin. Used for Briani and North Indian Vegetable dishes. It is roasted, ground and used sparingly as when sprinkled over North Indian Mutton Curry.

SARDINES: small mackerels, usually packed in tomato sauce, are misleadingly labelled 'sardines' in Malaysia and Singapore. They are much longer than, and different in flavour from European sardines, so if not using a Malaysian or Singaporean brand, buy mackerel, snoek or even herring in tomato sauce.

SHALLOTS: the Malay name, *bawang merah*, means 'red onion' and is a good description of these pinkish-purple, marble-sized onions. If shallots are not available, use big purple Bombay onions or, failing these, brown skinned onions. One big onion is roughly equivalent to 8-10 shallots.

SOYA SAUCE: two types are used: thin light soya sauce, and thick dark black soya sauce. As the flavours differ, be sure to use the one called for in the recipe.

SPRING ONIONS: slender green stalks with a white base. Do not confuse with shallots, which are small round pink onions.

TAMARIND: the dried pulp of the fruit from the tamarind tree (*asam*) is used to give fragrant sourness to many dishes. Sometimes slices of dried fruit (*asam keping or asam gelugor*) are used. Generally available in curry shops.

TURMERIC: the fresh or dried root of the turmeric plant is used for colour and flavour in many dishes. Dried powdered turmeric can be substituted: use about 1 teaspoon powder to 1cm ($\frac{1}{2}$in) fresh turmeric. Turmeric leaves are occasionally used as a herb; if these are not available, omit, as there is no substitute.

WHITE POPPY SEEDS: sand-like grains that are creamy white in colour, poppy seeds are used mainly as a thickening agent. If white poppy seeds (*kas kas*) are not available, try ground almonds.

YAM BEAN: a crunchy white vegetable called *bangkwang* with a flavour that is like a cross between an apple and a potato. Tinned water chestnuts are probably the best substitute.

Index

STEP BY STEP

We thank C.K.Tang for the use of crockery for photography

NOODLES AND SINGAPORE DISHES

Egg

Omelette with Minced Meat Filling	23

Fish

Fish Head Soup with Black Pepper	39
Ikan Belada	39

Garnishing

Cooked Coconut Crumbs	34
Ginger Pickle	35

Meat

Bamiah (Arab Dish)	30
Honeydew Fried Chicken	36
Stuffed Beef Roll	29

Noodles and Rice

Baked Macaroni	21
Bee Hoon Salado	24
Chicken Bee Hoon Briani Style	22
Chicken Macaroni in Tomato Broth	23
Fried Bee Hoon - Indian Style	21
Fried Beef Kwei Teow - Malay Style	23
Fried Kwei Teow	32
Fried Vegetarian Rice	22
Mee Serani	26
Mee Siam Lemak	34
Mee Soto	32

Sauces

Peanut Sauce Dressing	29
Sauce for Beef Roll	29

Soup

Indian Mutton Soup	28

Vegetables

Chye Sim with Straw Mushrooms and Carrots	28
Dry Chap Chye	34
Fried Poh Piah (Spring Rolls)	35
Kai Lan with Sliced Fish	26
Spicy Long Beans	39
Spinach with Shredded Beef	28

MALAYSIAN AND INDONESIAN DISHES

Appetisers, Sauces and Dips

Sambal Asam	54
Sambal Blacan	47
Sambal Cuka	52
Sambal Mangga	47
Serundeng (Spiced Grated Coconut)	42

Egg

Omelette	53

Meat

Ayam Panggang Gahru	54
Chicken Curry (Indonesian Style)	42
Fried Ox Lung	40
Malay Chicken Rice	57
Rendang Rempah	43
Sambal Goreng	43

Rice

Nasi Ambang	40
Steamed Nasi Uduk	52

Seafood

Asam Pedas Melaka (Kuah Lada)	47
Gulai Nanas	48
Ikan Bawal Cuka	50
Ikan Goreng	40
Ikan Masak Kuning	50
Ikan Panggang (Grilled Fish)	54
Opor Sotong	52
Otak Otak	52
Papaya with Shellfish	50
Sambal Prawns	53
Sambal Sardine with Green Mango	44
Sambal Sotong Kering	48
Sardine Salad	44
Sardine with Pineapple in Coconut Milk	44
Steamed Chilli Fish	58
Steamed Ikan Bilis Fritters	51

Tahu

Sambal Empat Sekawan	62
Steamed Tahu with Minced Chicken	61
Tahu Belado	61
Tahu Telor with Peanut Sauce	62
Taukwa with Vegetable and Chicken Filling	63
Tempe (Fermented Soya Bean Cake)	42

Vegetables

Bitter Gourd with Taukwa	48
Fried Kangkong with Blacan	53
Green Beans and Sweet Potato Leaves in Coconut Milk	54
Mixed Vegetables (Malay Style)	56
Nangka Lemak (Jack Fruit in Coconut Milk)	56
Potato Cutlets	43
Sambal Terong	43
Sayur Kangkong Keledek	47
Urap Taugeh	42
Young Corn and Mushroom in Coconut Milk	44

NORTH INDIAN DISHES

Chutney and Sambal

Coconut Sambal	70
Gajjar Chutney (Carrot Chutney)	67
Tomato Putchree	78

Egg

Egg Curry with Shrimps and Potatoes	72
Egg and Lamb (or Beef) Kebab	68

Lentils and Beans

Green Bean Dhal	76
Watery Dhal	66

Meat

Crispy Mutton Chops	66
Dried Mutton Chops	72
Kheema (Minced Meat Curry)	66
Minced Chicken Kebab	70
Minced Mutton Balls	76
Mutton Chops with Gravy	72
North Indian Chicken Curry	64
Sliced Mutton Curry with Cauliflower	77
Stuffed Chicken Legs	68
Tomato Chicken Curry	77

Rice and Chapati

Chapati	67
Kitchree Rice	73
Pilau Rice with Cashew Nuts	76
Savoury Rice with Curried Lamb	76

Vegetables

Alu (Potato Curry)	66
Egyptian Salata	70
Fried Potatoes	76
Okra Kheema	66
Vegetarian Kheema	73
Vegetarian Korma	75

SOUTH INDIAN DISHES

Appetisers, Pickles and Chutney

Lime Pickle	97
Pickle	94
Pineapple Putchree	90
Sambal Ikan Bilis with Coconut	90

Meat

Beef Samak	92
Chicken Coconut Milk Curry	83
Chicken Curry	87
Fried Mutton Curry	86
Hot Kerala Chicken Curry	87
Indian Dalcha	96
Mutton Curry	84
Mysore Fried Chicken	90
Spicy Fried Mutton	93

Rice and Roti

Indian Nasi Lemak	86
Nasi Briani	96
Roti Mariam	83
Tomato Rice	90

Seafood

Crab Curry	83
Fish Curry with Drumsticks	89
Fish Head Curry	83
Hot Prawn Curry	81
Salt Fish Curry	93

Soup and Gravy

Dhal Rasam	89
Rasam	83
Sothi	92

Vegetables

Carrots and Grated Coconut	89
Crispy Long Beans	87
Cucumber Salad	87
Fried Cabbage	83
Fried Long Beans with Grated Coconut	92
Fried Spinach	93

SANDWICHES AND COCKTAIL SAVOURIES

Chicken Kebab	98
Chilli Pakorhas (Chilli Fritters)	102
Fried Ikan Bilis	100
Green Chilli Sauce	100
Samosas	102
Satay Flavoured Fish Balls	101
Spicy Prawn Fritters	101
Spicy Squids	100
Tahu Balls	101
Vegetable Puffs (Epok-Epok Sayur)	100

Sandwiches

Chicken Salad Sandwich (Arab)	103
Roast Beef and Pickle Sandwich	103
Salata (Salad Sandwich)	103
Sindhi Sandwich	102
Spicy Scrambled Egg Sandwich	104

DESSERTS, SINGAPORE AND MALAYSIAN CAKES

Badam Halwa (Almond Sweet)	113
Chocolate Sponge Pudding	116
Gajjah Ki Halwa	114
Gulab Jamun (Milk Sweets in Syrup)	113
Kueh Jongkong	109
Kueh Keswi	111
Kueh Kochi Kuah	107
Kueh Lapis Beras	109
Kueh Lompang	112
Magic Jelly	117
Ondeh Ondeh Keledek (Sweet Potato Balls)	108
Orange Jelly	118
Penggat Pisang (Banana in Gula Melaka Syrup)	116
Pulot Serikaya	112
Rice Dough	109
Rice Pudding with White Syrup	108
Serikaya Beras (Steamed Rice-Custard Cake)	108
Sevian or Semiah	113
Ubi Cerah (Tapioca Chips Cooked in Gula Melaka)	108
Urap Pisang (Sliced Banana in Grated Coconut)	114

Notes

Notes

Notes